BILL STANLEY BOOKS &
THE FORGOTTEN FOUNDERS PRESENT

Historic Sites of Norwich From the Beginning

A GIFT TO THE CHILDREN OF NORWICH FROM THE FORGOTTEN FOUNDERS
ON NORWICH'S 350TH ANNIVERSARY

Published By
Bill Stanley Books & The Forgotten Founders

Graphic Design Services By
Jesse F. Carbone – Carbone Graphics

Associate Publisher & Editor
Denison N. Gibbs

Printing Services By
Corporate Forms & Printing, Inc.

**BILL STANLEY BOOKS &
THE FORGOTTEN FOUNDERS PRESENT**

Historic Sites of
Norwich
From the Beginning

**A GIFT TO THE CHILDREN OF NORWICH
FROM THE FORGOTTEN FOUNDERS
ON NORWICH'S 350TH ANNIVERSARY**

PREFACE

This book is published by The Forgotten Founders, a tax-free historical society with a single mission. That mission is to establish in Norwich a library for The Forgotten Founders – those men who served as President of the Continental Congress – ten of whom, under our first Constitution, the Articles of Confederation, were actually the first ten Presidents of the United States. We also intend to establish a center to study the first Constitution and its contributions to America as the foundation to our current Constitution.

Samuel Huntington was the first President under the Articles of Confederation in Congress Assembled. Huntington, and the other 13 men who served at the most critical time in the history of a young nation, have been virtually forgotten.

It is our intent to build a library for all of them in Norwich as the appropriate site because our Samuel Huntington was technically this country's first President.

This book is to be distributed to the various schools throughout Norwich, with the hope that teachers will set aside an hour a week to discuss it. Occasionally they may visit one of Norwich's many historic sites. For young people, there is a special thrill in seeing as well as reading about a part of the past. That is the special opportunity Norwich has to offer its students.

Historic Sites of Norwich From the Beginning is my gift to the young people of Norwich on the occasion of Norwich's 350th anniversary. The cost has been underwritten by The Forgotten Founders of Norwich.

FORWARD

Americans, some cynical observer once said, think history is something that happens to other people. He meant that most of the time, Americans concentrate on the present and the future, which have always been rich in possibility and hope. But some places have a history that is too important to ignore. Norwich is one of those places.

Over the centuries the city has produced many men and women who played important roles in the larger drama of the nation's history. Even more impressive, Norwich's past extends backward to the decades and even centuries before there was a nation. Its history includes the first encounters between red men and white men on this continent.

Norwich is fortunate to have had in its past people who realized the importance of this history and did their best to preserve its memory. Few of these Norwich patriots have done more in this often difficult task than Bill Stanley. His books and newspaper columns have rescued scores of events and people for future generations to ponder and appreciate. In this book he has summed up his efforts with a wonderful combination of pictures and text.

Someday soon, I am confident that Norwich will help Bill achieve his most ambitious dream – to establish a Library of the Forgotten Founders to preserve the genius, self sacrifice and wisdom of the presidents of the Continental Congress, the men who led the country during the struggle for our independence. The example of Norwich's own Samuel Huntington, one of the most distinguished members of this gallery of heroes, has inspired Bill Stanley to propose this project. He has the enthusiastic backing of many of America's leading historians.

Thomas Fleming

Past President of the Society of American Historians

A Message From The Forgotten Founders

In the beginning was the rugged land – scape cut by swift streams from upland rolling plains all coming together at the juncture of two meandering rivers that empty together into one very large tidal river. Such was the fruitful terrain that welcomed various wandering Indian tribal colonies over the centuries. Then around 1600 A.D. a Mohegan from what is today central Connecticut was married to a royal Pequot princess; he was granted the aforementioned tract that the Pequots called "SONDAHQUE."

In time a son known as Uncas claims this territory and renames the land "MOHEGAN." Frequent attacks from the Narragansett tribe under Chief Miantonomah (1643) who was captured in a foot chase by Tantequeison and subsequently put to death, and Pessacus, brother of Miantonomah, (1645 and 1647) lead to an alliance between Uncas and English settlements in Saybrook and Pequot (New London). This alliance brings permanent protection for Uncas and his people and creates a favorable relationship for new colonists.

Forward to June and again on August 15, 1659 when a delegation of 35 proprietors from Saybrook led by Capt. John Mason and Rev. James Fitch execute deeds conveying from Uncas for 70 pounds a 9-Mile Square (81 square miles) of Mohegan land for a new colony. Immediately work parties arrive to survey house lots and cart paths along 5 miles of the east bank of Yantic River above The Falls.

In the spring of 1660 the actual settlement of MOHEGAN occurs with residents arriving en-masse along with goods and cattle.

Background On The Cover Photo

On July 2, 1907, Buffalo Bill's Wild West Show visited Norwich, and on the morning of that day Colonel William F. Cody (Buffalo Bill) accompanied by Chiefs Rocky Bear and Iron Tail of the Sioux tribe and one hundred other Indians made a pilgrimage to the "Royal Burying Ground of the Mohegans." Here the Indians formed a circle around the monument of Uncas and chanted a war song. Colonel Cody placed a large wreath of flowers on the grave of the great Sachem, and taps were sounded by a member of the cavalry who was present with the party.

TABLE OF CONTENTS

Bill Stanley Books and The Forgotten Founders express their great gratitude for certain illustrations and text taken from an earlier publication, "Norwich Historic Homes and Families."

East Great Plains
Mohegan Battleground

Plaque sponsored by the Mohegan Tribe

Located on 574 New London Turnpike (Three Rivers Community College)

This boulder was dedicated in 1927 to commemorate the Great Plains Battle.

In 1643, the Narragansett Sachem, Miantonomo, raised an army of 900 and marched against Uncas. The war party was discovered coming down the Quinnebaug. Mohegan runners were sent to warn Uncas at Fort Shantok and Mohegans at nearby villages. The Mohegan warriors hastily gathered and advanced to the Great Plain where Uncas confronted Miantonomo and challenged him to single-handed combat. Miantonomo refused and said that since his warriors had come prepared to fight, they would do battle. At hearing this, Uncas dropped to the ground, and his warriors, at a prearranged plan threw the Narragansetts into flight. They were unable to rally their men from this suprise, and they were chased to the brink of the Yantic River where many lives were lost. The remainder were pursued to Sachem Plain by the Mohegans. Miantonomo was captured and held for Uncas. Also caught were a brother of Miantonomo and two sons of the Narragansett sachem, Canonicus. After a stay with Uncas of several months, the authorities demanded Miantonomo be sent to Hartford to await their judgement.

Miantonomo Monument
Plaque sponsored by the Mohegan Tribe
Located on Elijah Street

This stone structure was erected to commemorate the capture near here of Miantonomo, the Great Chief of the Narragansetts by Uncas, Chief of the Mohegans.

After being captured along with some of his leaders at the Battle of Great Plains, Miantonomo and his warriors were taken to Shantok by Uncas. He was treated well but Uncas finally was ordered to surrender him to the English so they could decide the Narragansett's fate. Miantonomo was kept in prison for about six weeks, and then the authorities had him released to Uncas and his warriors with orders to execute him away from any of the settlers' towns, so Narragansett reprisals would not fall on their heads. Hopkins, Whiting, and John Mason, along with eight soldiers, had accompanied the Mohegans to see that the sentence was carried out and to defend Uncas in case the Narragansetts sought to avenge Miantonomo's execution. Miantonomo was executed with a hatchet in a single stroke wielded by Wawecqua, the brother of Uncas, somewhere on the path between Hartford and Norwich.*

This single act would prevent the Mohegans and Narragansetts from ever uniting against the colonists.

---

* Benjamin Trumbull, writing 175+ years after the fact, says that the execution was at Sachem's Plain but none of the original documents have "Sachem's Plain" as an execution place. Recent scholars tend to agree that Miantonomo was probably executed along the path between Hartford and Norwich, probably sooner rather than later, to avoid the possibility of the Narragansetts swooping down and freeing their sachem *en route*; and well away from any settlement, in agreement with the United Colony's orders.

Norwich Corner Marker

Plaque sponsored by the Mohegan Tribe
Located off Route 12, Plainfield

David Oat standing by the ancient Norwich N.E. corner marker.

When the town of Norwich was founded in 1659, the boundary markers for the land were commonly referred to as the "Nine Miles Square." According to Daniel Phillips' *History of Griswold*, in 1916 the Anne Brewster Fanning Chapter of the Daughters of the American Revolution took it upon themselves to identify and restore the ancient Norwich N.E. corner marker located in Griswold/Plainfield. In 1734, ancient records indicated, a tall stone post was set to replace a pile of stones which earlier surveys had identified as the N.E. boundary of Norwich. Years passed, the old stone marker was left leaning over after many years of neglect. Using old town records, the ancient boundary marker was relocated. A careful comparison of the location of this stone post with the original records, revealed the unquestionable identifying marks set down both in the renewal of bounds in 1685 and in Avery's survey of 1734. Following restoration and relettering, the marker was permanently reset in concrete. On this site in May of 1917, members of the Anne Brewster Fanning Chapter of the Daughters of the American Revolution held a ceremony attended by about 100 people.

In May of this year, I talked to Erwin Goldstein, president of the Griswold Historical Society, and asked if he knew where the Norwich boundary marker was located. He said that he had seen it about 25 years ago and perhaps, with some hunting around, maybe the two of us could relocate it. We drove out of Jewett City together. We parked and followed a set of railroad tracks off Route 12 in Plainfield for quite a distance. We then cut off into a heavily wooded area. I expected the old stone post, if it still existed would be lying on the ground under the leaves after all these years. But, after searching for about 20 minutes, there it was, still standing, with the old inscription easily readable. For a couple of old historians, finding this old piece of history really made our day.

The inscription reads:

YE
ANCIENT
NORWICH
N.E. CORNER
BOUND.
1659-1917
D.A.R.

Text by David Oat.

Yantic Falls

Plaque sponsored by the City of Norwich
Located on Yantic Street

The Yantic Falls

Yantic Falls, known as Indian Leap, was a favorite encampment of the Mohegan Indians. In 1643, Uncas, Sachem of the Mohegans, led his warriors in the famous battle against their rival tribe the Narragansetts. During the battle, the Narragansetts were pursued by the Mohegans. Legend has it that a band of Narragansetts, unfamiliar with the territory, unknowingly reached the high treacherous escarpment of the Falls. The Narragansetts, rather than surrender, attempted to leap the chasm. Unsuccessful, they plunged to their death into the abyss below.

The Yantic Falls became the genesis for industrial development in Norwich. Industry and the use of waterpower in this area dates back to he development of a grist mill in the 1600s by John Elderkin. Industrial development continued to grow until the early 1900s. Later industries at the Falls included paper making, cotton, and nails.

The improvements of the Yantic Falls Park have been made in part through a grant by the State of Connecticut, Department of Environmental Protection and in part by funding through the City of Norwich.

Uncas Monument

Plaque sponsored by WICH/WCTY

Located on Sachem Street in the Royal Indian Burial Ground

"Buffalo Bill" Cody made a pilgrimage to the Uncas Monument in 1907.

This monument commemorates the final resting place of Uncas (circa 1606-1683). The monument was dedicated by President Andrew Jackson in 1833. The fenced area is what remains of a much larger original Indian burial ground.

Uncas became Sachem or Chief of the Mohegans. A splintered but related faction of the Pequots, after a rivalry occurred over succession rights with Sassacus, the Pequot Sachem. The Pequots were a powerful tribe of Algonkian stock in the mid-seventeenth century who subjected the local tribes. They controlled southeastern Connecticut territorially and economically. Since the fighting strength of the Connecticut colony was drawn from but 250-300 men, Uncas became an important ally.

Serious incidents, including a punitive expedition by the English, inflamed passions between the Pequots and English. But after the Pequots killed 8 men and women during spring planting, the colony mounted an offensive under Capt. John Mason. Uncas with 70 warriors, joined Mason's 90 men. Narragansett and Nehantics supplemented these, and the forces surprised the Pequot fort at Mystic, Connecticut in June 1637. In the struggle, Mason fired the fort. A large number of people were massacred in the conflagration. With the attacking force in retreat, and the larger body of Pequots unscathed at nearby Fort Hill, the Pequots counterattacked; then elected to flee. Sassacus sought refuge with the Mohawks in New York, but they killed him and sent his head to the English.

A shrewd leader, Uncas routed the Narragansett, powerful tribe from Rhode Island, after they attacked the greatly outnumbered Mohegans near here in 1643. Two years later, a Narragansett siege of the Mohegan stronghold at Shantok was defeated.

Subsequently, the Mohegans emerged as one of the most powerful tribes in New England. They were largely responsible for keeping Connecticut relatively free of the terror of King Philip's War, fought to stop English expansion. It was the bloodiest conflict (1675-1676) between Indians and English settlers in the 17th century. The Mohegans, under Oweneco, Uncas's eldest son, with Pequots and English helped defeat Philip's ally, the Narragansett.

The Mohegans also fought with the colonists during the revolution. Their descendents reside in Norwich today.

Royal Mohegan Burial Ground

Plaque sponsored by the Mohegan Tribe
Located on Sachem Street

YOU NOW STAND ON THE SITE OF THE MOHEGAN TRIBE'S ROYAL BURIAL GROUND. HERE REST THE REMAINS OF MOHEGANS WHOSE GRAVES WERE DESECRATED IN THEIR ANCESTRAL SOIL. MAY THEY REST IN PEACE, NOW AND FOREVER.

The Royal Mohegan Burying Ground monument with 13 pillars representing the 13 moons of a year.
(top-right) The epithet written by Council of Elders Chairman, John Henry Clark.

For untold centuries, the rulers and their families of the Mohegan Tribe were buried here. Early accounts tell of the deceased being carried over in a boat from where he had dwelled and being carried up the ravine, like a deer, bound to a long pole. After suitable rites, many were interred along with their favorite possessions to accompany them on their long journey through eternity. The original sixteen acres has diminished through the years, and when the last burial, that of Charles Bohema at the age of 59 in 1870, less than 1/8 of an acre remained.

In 1998, this land and that which was owned by the Masonic Temple came back into the hands of the Mohegan Tribe. Demolition of the structures on this land started on October 10, 2006. In August 2008, the land was rededicated to the memory of all the Mohegans who were buried here.

The Norwichtown Green

Plaque sponsored by The State of Connecticut
Located at the intersection of Town Street, West Town Street,
& East Town Street

The Norwichtown Green

In 1659 the Mohegan chief Uncas sold to settlers led by Major John Mason and the Reverend James Fitch "nine miles square," part of which became Norwich. According to Frances M. Caulkins's *History of Norwich*, "At the end of the first century . . . the church no longer necessary as a look-out post of the town, came down from the hill, and took its position at the corner of the Green . . . the place where trades, merchandize, public business, military exercises, shows, sports, festivals, and the general enterprise of the town, found a center."

"The County Jail stood on the north side at the foot of the hill; the Court House was in the open area; the Post Office not far from the meeting house . . . taverns, schools, and shops alternating with private dwellings around the border."

Opposition to British rule increased over the next few years and t he residents erected Liberty Tree, "a lofty pole . . . decked with standards and appropriate devices . . . Here almost daily, people assembled to hear the news, make speeches, and encourage each other in the determination to resist the oppression."

Bean Hill

Plaque sponsored by the Norwich Grange & Norwich Tenpin Bowl
Located on West Town Street at Route 395

Bean Hill

Once upon a time in Norwich . . . Bean Hill, at the northwest end of the original English settlement of Norwich, was named for the traditional New England dish of baked beans. In 1729, the town set aside the green for public use. Bean Hill soon became an important center of trade. Stores exchanged goods for farm products. Taverns provided lodging and entertainment. Local crafts flourished, producing a variety of wares, including pottery, hats, leather, barrels, nails, and woodwork. Woolen mills were established in the early 1800s. Bean Hillers were active in the religious and political ferment of the 1700s and 1800s. Dissenters from the Congregational Church met at Bean Hill in 1745. The first Episcopal services in town were held here in 1738. Early Methodists also worshipped here. Political speeches and public gatherings were held under an elm on the green. Major John Durkee was a leader of the Sons of Liberty, opposing the British Stamp Act in 1765. Aaron Cleveland opposed slavery in 1774. David Ruggles, an African American born here in 1810, was a major figure in the Underground Railroad. Another native, David Case, was Norwich's first casualty in the Civil War.

Yantic

Plaque sponsored by the Yantic Volunteer Fire Department
Located on 151 Yantic Road

Yantic Fire Engine Company

The village of Yantic, located in the City of Norwich lies in the northwest corner bounded by the towns of Bozrah and Franklin. These towns were once part of the original nine-mile square purchased from the Mohegan Indians in 1659, and were known first as New Concord and West Farms. These areas were set off from Norwich and made separate towns in 1786.

Captain Erastus Williams renamed West Farm and called it Yantic. This name was derived from the Mohegan Indian origin, " Yantick," meaning Little River. Williams built the Yantic Mill, the Church, the Mill Houses, Store, and Fire Department. In 1847 the Mill owner petitioned the Connecticut General Assembly for a Charter for a Fire Company in the Village of Yantic. In July of 1847 the General Assembly granted the Charter to Erastus Williams, and the Yantic Fire Engine Company No. 1 was created.

The Church was established in 1853, and the existing stone building was dedicated on June 22, 1902. The son of Erastus, Winslow Williams, oversaw the construction of the double arch stone bridge which led to his residence, "Rockclyffe." Mr. Williams was a personal friend of President William Howard Taft who visited on July 5, 1909 to celebrate Norwich's 250th Anniversary.

Leffingwell Inn

Plaque sponsored by Mr. Thomas Leffingwell Pulling
Located on 348 Washington Street

(left) Leffingwell Inn Museum. (top) The Leffingwell Inn today.

Once upon a time in Norwich, there was a two-room building owned by the Stephen Backus family in 1675. It later passed to Thomas Leffingwell, the son of Lt. Thomas Leffingwell, and in 1701 he was given permission to open an inn. There followed two major additions to the original building to provide space for that use.

Thomas's son, Benajah, succeeded his father as an innkeeper and, in turn, Benajah's son, Christopher Leffingwell, continued in that business. Christopher Leffingwell, Norwich industrialist, entrepreneur, merchant and patriot distinguished himself for his contribution of provisions to the success of the American Revolution. En route to Providence during the war, General George Washington dined at the Leffingwell Inn and met with patriots from the region.

The Leffingwell Inn originally was located at the corner of Harland Road and Washington Street. In 1957 it was doomed for demolition to make way for the new Connecticut Turnpike connector. Fortunately, Philip A. Johnson, President of the Society of the Founders of Norwich, with the help of then Governor Abraham Ribicoff and State Highway Commissioner Newman E. Argraves, made possible its purchase by the State Highway Department. It was then deeded to the Society of the Founders of Norwich with the provision that the Society maintain the Inn as an historic site. At a cost of $100,000, it was moved to the present location at 348 Washington Street, where it is regularly opened to the public as one of New England's finest examples of colonial architecture and furnishings.

Meeting House Rocks

Located on West Town Street

The Meeting House Rocks

MEETING-HOUSE ROCKS

IN 1673 ON THE SUMMIT OF THESE ROCKS WAS ERECTED THE SECOND MEETING HOUSE BUILT IN THE TOWN OF NORWICH, WHICH SERVED ALSO AS A WATCH TOWER AGAINST THE INDIANS . . . . .

The rocky ledge west of the Norwichtown Congregational Church was the site in 1675 of the second meeting house in Norwich. The place served a three-fold purpose as a place of worship, as a watchtower against the Indians, and as a garrison post. It is now a site for outdoor worship by the First Congregational Church.

John Mason Home Lot

Plaque sponsored by the Gernon Trust
Located on 90 Town Street

The early life of John Mason in England (born circa 1600-01) is obscure. A Puritan, he served as an officer under Sir Thomas Fairfax, in the Netherlands against Spain. He made the 63 day passage to the Massachusetts Bay colony with Reverend Wareham's party in 1630. One of the few experienced military men, he was elected captain at Dorchester, and eventually helped found Windsor, Connecticut, where the Connecticut River Indians had invited settlement.

In 1636, the first Pequot war began in New England, between Indians and the English. The colony had but a few hundred English inhabitants. Mason commanded a contingent of 90 soldiers, and with the principal aid of Uncas and the Mohegans, he defeated the powerful Pequot nation in 1637. Disobeying orders, he made strategic decisions of his own, which helped gain victory over a more numerous enemy. He lost 2 dead and 20 wounded. The Pequots lost hundreds. Many warriors and noncombatants alike perished when one of their forts was burned by Mason. The Pequots then retreated from Connecticut. Mason said of Uncas . . . "He was a great friend and did great service."

Major Mason was the chief military officer in the colony for 35 years. He was magistrate and major at Windsor for 8 years. He married his second wife, Anne Peck, after the death of his first wife, and had altogether 8 children. A son, John Jr., was mortally wounded in King Philip's War (another English/Indian struggle) in 1675. For the next 12 years he was placed in charge of a fort in Saybrook. In 1660, with his son-in-law, the Rev. James Fitch, he founded Norwich. During the first eight years, he was made deputy governor, and for two years was acting governor while Gov. Winthrop was in England seeking Connecticut's charter from King Charles. He died January 30, 1672.

Founders Cemetery

Plaque sponsored by Mr. Thomas Leffingwell Pulling
Located on Lee Avenue

Mason Monument in Post & Gager Burial Ground (~1909).

Once upon a time in Norwich, upon the death of a most prominent lady, the new community realized they needed a cemetery. It was March, 1661 when Mrs. Sarah Post passed away. She was buried on the home lot of her husband, Thomas Post.

Norwich, as an incorporated city, was just two years old, but not far from this cemetery a hardy race of Puritans established their new community known as Norwich. "They were a fearless, resolute people. They were bound by a common faith. They were an associated body both in civil and ecumenical capacity," and when they came upon the ground where they built their church, they started a new Christian settlement, first called Mohegan, but later, in 1659, incorporated as Norwich.

It was December 16, 1661 that the town purchased a burying place of Thomas Post. It was a parcel of land 8 rods one way and 5-1/2 rods the other way in the home lot of said Thomas Post. It was often referred to as the Post Gager Burial Ground. It is now designated as The Founders' Cemetery.

In this sacred soil are buried the founders of the City of Norwich, their wives and other family members: Rev. James Fitch, Mayor John Mason, Thomas Adgate, Robert Allyn, William Backus, John Baldwin, John Birchard, Thomas Bliss, Morgan Bowers, Richard Edgarton, Francis Griswold, Christopher Huntington, Simon Huntington, William Hyde, Samuel Hyde, Thomas Leffingwell, John Olmstead, John Pease, John Post, Thomas Post, John Reynolds, Jonathan Royce, Nehemiah Smith, Thomas Tracy, Thomas Bingham, John Bradford, John Gager, Thomas Howard, Thomas Waterman, John Tracy, John Calkins, Stephen Gifford, Josiah Reed, Richard Wallis, Stephen Backus, Richard Hendys and Robert Wade.

Bradford-Huntington Home

Located on 16 Huntington Lane

The Bradford-Huntington House

Thought to be Norwich's oldest house, this house is one of the three remaining structures built by a founder. It was built in different sections at various periods. In 1691 Simon Huntington, Jr., purchased the land and "new dwelling house." Additions to the house were attributed to him. In 1719 Simon's son, Joshua, obtained the homestead. The heavy, plain, box cornice, the attic overhang, and the pediments over the end windows are all primitive features of the 1719 addition.

The broad rear ell along Huntington Lane was built by Joshua's son, General Jabez Huntington, a wealthy West Indian trader who came into possession of the property in 1745. He installed much of the fine paneling. Some of the shutters have heart-shaped openings, and the double door on the ell is studded with nails in diamond patterns. The interior hardware is notable. Leaden sash weights from this old house were cast into bullets during the Revolution.

General Jabez Huntington was born in 1719. After graduating from college in 1741 he entered into commercial life in Norwich, added largely to his father's ample fortune, and at the beginning of the Revolution, owned a large number of vessels engaged in foreign trade. Though fully aware of the risk in his business, he was an ardent participant in the War of Independence. He gave largely of his fortune for the cause.

General Jedediah Huntington was one of their sons, born August 4, 1743. In 1741-2 he married Elizabeth, daughter of Samuel and Elizabeth (Tracy) Backus. She died in 1745. He then married Hannah, daughter of the Reverend Ebenezer Williams of Pomfret.

According to Crofut's *Guide to Historic Sites*, George Washington spent the night of April 8, 1775 at this house. Lafayette is said to have been entertained here during some of visits to Norwich.

Colonial Cemetery

Plaque sponsored by the Major J. D. Robertson Family
Located on 40 East Town Street, with an entrance also from 85 Town Street

Entrance to the Colonial Cemetery (The Old Burying Ground).

The old burying ground at the end of the Old Cemetery Lane was purchased in 1699 and in 1796 an addition was acquired. The gates shown here were placed at the entrance to the latter purchase. The gates are called the Amos Hallum Hubbard Gates and were acquired from the Palmer Smith estate by the Daughters of the American Revolution. They were dedicated on July 5, 1903. Originally the gates guarded the entrance to the Amos Hallum Hubbard Mansion, built in 1832. The Mansion was torn down in 1903 to make way for the present Post Office on Main Street in downtown Norwich.

The iron from which these gates were molded is supposed to have come from the famous Salisbury Iron Mines in Litchfield County, Connecticut. The Salisbury Mines produced iron for Revolutionary War cannons, cannon balls, the anchors for the frigate *Constitution* ("Old Ironsides"), and the chain that blockaded the Hudson River.

The Colonial Cemetery

A tablet located inside the Colonial Cemetery. The inscripton reads:
IN MEMORY OF
TWENTY FRENCH SOLDIERS
WHO, SERVING UNDER
LAFAYETTE,
DIED WHILE IN CAMP AT
NORWICH TOWN 1778

Christopher Huntington, Jr., Home

Located on 410 Washington Street

The Christopher Huntington, Jr., House

Christopher Huntington, 2nd, or Deacon Christopher as he was frequently referred to, was born November 1, 1660, and was the first male child born in Norwich. He was the son of Christopher and Ruth (Rockwell) Huntington. In 1681 he married Sarah, daughter of Thomas Adgate. She died in 1705-06 and he then married Mrs. Judith (Stevens) Brewster, the widow of Jonathan Brewster.

Christopher was a deputy and frequently chosen as a townsman. He served as town clerk, succeeding Richard Bushnell from 1698 to 1702. He was an expert surveyor and frequently settled questions of boundary. He was appointed a deacon in 1695-6.

He had a total of eleven children. He died in 1735 and the property was inherited by sons, John and Jeremiah. John subsequently deeded his portion of the properties to Jeremiah and when he left Norwich, he sold the property to Samuel Avery.

African-American Heritage

The house built by former slave, Guy Druck, at 76 Church Street, and site of the African-American Heritage plaque.

In the late 1600's and 1700's, Norwich was an important colonial seaport trading with the West Indies. Slaves were imported to southeastern Connecticut from the West Indies during this period. They became personal servants, laborers, and craftsmen. By 1756, the black community numbered 223. Many had purchased their own freedom or had been freed by their owners. Former slave, Guy Druck, a blacksmith, built the house at 76 Church Street in the 1750's. His skills were renowned and actively sought by ship builders for components such as anchors. Blacks from Norwich, such as Leb Quy, fought in the American Revolution. The first public outcry against slavery in Norwich was published in the Norwich Packet in 1174. Connecticut later passed legislation to gradually abolish slavery in 1784.

In the 19th century, black settlement centered on Jail Hill, where a thriving community existed by the mid-century. Discriminated against for employment in the mills, Norwich's black residents worked on the docks, railroads, steamboats, and in hotels. Many, like escaped slave James Linsley Smith, a shoemaker, were engaged in crafts. Others owned restaurants and small businesses.

Norwich was on one of the routes of the underground railroad; the secret network helped escaped slaves from the south reach safety in Canada. David Ruggles, an important "conductor" based in New York, was a native of Norwich.

In the 20th century, new immigrants from the American south and Cape Verde Islands settled in Norwich thus enriching the life of the community.

Jesse Brown Tavern

Located on 77 East Town Street

The Jesse Brown Tavern, now home of United Community and Family Services. (right) Close-up of the iron fence.

Jesse Brown married Anna Rudd, daughter of Nethaniel and Mary (Backus) Rudd of Franklin, Connecticut in 1769. They had six children. He participated in the Revolution by officiating as the Governor's Post. As express agent and confidential messenger, he relayed the news of the occupation of Philadelphia by the British under Lord Howe. In 1781 he married his wife's cousin, Lucy Rudd, daughter of Daniel and Mary (Metcalf) Rudd.

In 1790 he was licensed to open a tavern. He became the stage contractor and established lines between Boston and New York via Providence and Norwich.

On Wednesday evening, August 1, 1797 President John Adams and his wife were guests at the Jesse Brown Tavern. He was welcomed by the Matross Company in full uniform and honored with a sixteen-gun salute.

One of his daughters, Ann, married John Vernet who built the lovely home located at 118 Washington Street. The famous Vernet grape were first cultivated in the garden of Jesse Brown's Tavern. Mr. Brown died in 1818 in Wilkes Barre, Pennsylvania, where he lived with the Vernet family.

Extensively altered, it has been known as the Rock Nook Home for Children. The United Workers, the present owner, constitute the organized charities of Norwich and serve as The Public Health Agency. It is now home to the United Community and Family Services.

Silversmith & Schoolhouse On The Green

Plaque sponsored by Margot Hacker Gibbs

Located on 73 (Silversmith) & 69 (Schoolhouse) East Town Street

(top) Silversmith & (bottom) Schoolhouse on the Green.

Once upon a time in Norwich, about 1773, Joseph Carpenter, II, a clockmaker and goldsmith, has this building constructed. It served him and his brother, Gardner, in jewelry, clocks, engravings and mercantile. It is thought to be the only remaining wooden silversmith/goldsmith structure surviving in New England.

At the close of the American Revolution, in the same year that the Paris Treaty was signed, 1783, this brick schoolhouse was constructed on the Green. It was named for Dr. Daniel Lathrop who left a legacy of 500 pounds for an endowed free grammar school. Later it was occupied by the Noah Webster Literary Association and is one of the earliest brick schoolhouses still standing in the state.

Diah Manning Home

Plaque sponsored by the Major J. D. Robertson Family
Located on 85 Town Street

The Diah Manning House

Samuel Manning, born in 1723, married Anne Winship in 1746. He died in 1783 and his widow, Anne, daughter Eunice and son Diah inherited the house. Diah was born in 1760. In 1784 he married Anna Gifford, daughter of James and Susanna (Hubbard) Gifford. He and his brother, Roger, served as drummers in the Revolutionary War. In 1775 Roger was in Colonel Israel Putnam's regiment and Diah in the 8th Regiment under Colonel Jedediah Huntington. At Valley Forge in 1778 both brothers were chosen to be in Washington's Body Guard, Diah being designated Drum Major. Diah carried to Major André his last breakfast on the morning of his execution.

Diah's family was extremely kind to a young mulatto from Haiti who was captured by the Americans. His name was Jean Pierre Boyer who became president of the Republic of Haiti and later sent a present of $400 each to the widows of Consider Sterry and Diah Manning in return for their kindness to him in his captivity.

East District School
Located on 365 Washington Street

The East District School

The exact date on this building is not known but it is probably late 18th century. Lydia Huntley Sigourney recalls attending school there as a four-year-old. In 1798 Consider Sterry opened an evening school for instruction in writing and bookkeeping. He also taught mathematics, surveying without plotting, and laying out of lands. He taught sea-going men to obtain longitude at sea by lunar observations and how to find latitude by sun's altitude. The only prerequisite for these courses was that the person be able to read.

Besides his wok on lunar observations he and his brother published a book on mathematics with Nathan Daboll. He edited a system of practical navigation entitled "The Seaman's Universal Daily Assistant" nearly 300 pages long. He also wrote several small treatises and political articles. All of this was attained with no training as he was completely self-taught.

Consider Sterry was born in 1761 and was the brother of Rev. John Sterry. In 1780 he married Sabra Park, daughter of Silas and Sarah (Ayer) Park of Preston. This wife died in 1794 and he married Mary (Norman) Hazen, a widow. He had 17 children.

Lathrop Home

Located on 380 Washington Street

The Lathrop House

This site is the John Olmstead home lot, later the Samuel Lathrop home lot, inherited by Daniel Lathrop, Samuel's son, in 1774. The original home was burned in February 1745. Recent restoration disclosed charred lumber, indicating that the original house forms part of the present structure.

Dr. Daniel Lathrop was the son of Thomas and Lydia (Abel) Lathrop. He was born in 1712 and 1744 married Jerusha Talcott, daughter of Governor Joseph and Abigail (Clarke) Talcott of Hartford. In 1733 he graduated from Yale and went to Europe to study "Chirurgery," but started the first apothecary shop between Boston and New York. Dr. Daniel died in 1782.

This house was the home of many famous persons including Lydia Huntley Sigourney, poetess, born here in 1791; Daniel Coit Gilman (1831-1908), noted educator; John Olmstead, first physician in Norwich, and Samuel Lathrop, early settler.

A Note On Benedict Arnold

In his youth, Benedict Arnold served five years of indentured servitude and lived in this house. Benedict Arnold came from an excellent family background. His grandfather was Governor of Rhode Island. His mother was the daughter of a prominent citizen, and her epitaph states that "she was a pattern of piety, patience, and virtue."

Many tales have circulated about Arnold's wild, undisciplined childhood, but virtually none is true. His father's health problems caused young Benedict to leave school and become an apprentice to his mother's cousins, Daniel and Joshua Lathrop. Those two Norwichites taught him the apothecary's trade and then helped set him up in business in New Haven, Connecticut. There, Arnold became a prosperous merchant, heavily involved in the West Indies trade.

The Revolution fostered Arnold's remarkable talents as a daring commander on land and water. He fought courageously at Ticonderoga, Quebec, Lake Champlain, and at the pivotal battles of Saratoga. He repelled a British force at Danbury, Connecticut for which the Continental Congress finally named him a major general. George Washington praised Arnold as his fighting general.

Wounded seriously at Quebec and then again at Saratoga, and seeing how poorly Congress supported its army, Arnold started to doubt the merits of the patriotic cause. Problems with local officials in Philadelphia during 1778, after Washington named him military governor there, added to his growing disillusionment. After a vicious public attack on his character, Arnold opened negotiations with the British. He believed the Revolution had lost its way and would collapse, and he hoped to lead the people in settling their differences with the Crown short of independence.

In September 1780, amid a failed plot to turn patriot defenses at West Point, New York over to the British, Arnold defected. The British awarded him the rank of brigadier and indemnified him for his property losses, although more had been requested.

As a British officer, Arnold led attacks on Richmond, Virginia, and in September 1781 on New London, Connecticut. The massacre of American soldiers at Fort Griswold across the Thames River that day, as well as the burning of New London, further increased patriotic enmity toward Arnold. He was not at Fort Griswold but was in overall command of the troops who attacked that bastion.

After the war, Arnold resumed his mercantile career, trading out of Canada and England. He never quite enjoyed the prosperity of his earlier years. Arnold died in London in June 1801, aged 60 years, his name, despite his invaluable service to the patriot cause, to become synonymous with treason.

His remains are interred at St. Mary's of Battersea Church in London with his wife, Margaret Shippen Arnold, and daughter, Sophia.

Text by Professor James Kirby Martin, author, historian, professor of history.

Lathrop Pharmacy

Located on 377 Washington Street

The Lathrop Pharmacy

Dr. Joshua Lathrop, the son of Thomas and Lydia (Abel) Lathrop, was born in 1723. In 1748 he married Hannah Gardiner, daughter of David and Rachel (Schellinx) Gardiner of Gardiner's Island. She died in 1760 and in 1761 he married Mercy Eels, daughter of Rev. Nathaniel and Mercy (Cushing) Eels of Stonington.

He graduated from Yale in 1743 and joined his brother, Dr. Daniel Lathrop, in the first drug store in Connecticut and actually the first one between Boston and New York.

Notes: This house was built in two main parts, a saltbox section and a three-bay Georgian section. It is believed the saltbox section was the first part built. Interesting features: Original fireplaces, including a nine-foot cooking fireplace; original paneling – most in good condition; a smoking chamber in the attic and a cold storage chamber in the cellar (both built into the chimney), also an attached woodshed.

Jedediah Huntington Home

Located on 23 East Town Street

General Jedediah Huntington House. Marker on egg-shaped glacial boulder found on Jedediah Huntington Home lot.

General Jedediah Huntington was born in 1743, the son of General Jabez and Elizabeth (Backus) Huntington. He graduated from Harvard College with honors, and then went into business with his father. He became a valiant soldier during the Revolution and fought courageously during the Battle of Bunker Hill, from which he emerged a Colonel.

After the Battle of Bunker Hill he fought in New York and Pennsylvania. He endured the hardships of Valley Forge and helped repulse the British at Danbury, Connecticut, in 1776. In 1777, at General Washington's request, he was made a Brigadier General and at the end of the war received the commission of Major General. After the war he served many important positions such as High Sheriff for the County of New London, Judge of Probate for the district of Norwich, First Alderman of the city of Norwich, one of the representatives of the town in the State Legislature. He was one of the founders of the Order of Cincinnati.

He married Faith Trumbull in 1766, daughter of Governor Jonathan Trumbull of Lebanon, Connecticut. They had one son, Jabez. After her death he married Ann Moore of New York. They had seven children.

General Jedediah Huntington was the first collector of U.S. Customs under the Federal Constitution. He was appointed in 1789 by General Washington, removed to New London and built a home there at the corner of Broad and Washington Streets. He died in New London in 1818 at the age of 75. He was initially buried in New London but his remains were later removed to Norwich and buried in the old burying grounds near the Green.

This house contains a very handsome staircase with mahogany rail and rope balusters.

Lowthorpe Meadows

Plaque sponsored by the Lothropp Family Foundation
Located on 382 Washington Street

(left) Lowthorpe Meadows. (right) The gate to Lowthorpe Meadows.

This plot of land, now known as the Lowthorpe Meadows, was deeded in 1905 to Wallace S. Allis, Caroline T. Gilman, Elizabeth Gilman, George H. Gilman, Charlotte C. Gulliver, William H. Palmer and Herbert L. Yerrington. The deed reads as follows:

Dear Friends,
   For the consideration of the love and good will that we have to the inhabitants of the town of Norwich, we desire to give to you and your successors for ever the greater part of the land owned by us on the west side of Washington Street, as shown by the accompanying plan, that it may be kept perpetually as a free open space for the public good, unencumbered by dwelling houses, barns or any nuisance whatever.

Emily S. Gilman
Louisa G. Lane
Norwich, Conn. Nov. 30, 1905

The name Lowthorpe comes from the old English form of Lothrop or Lathrop. In 1745, Thomas Lathrop owned this property. This same Thomas Lathrop was an ancestor of the Gilman family.

Hannah Arnold Gravesite

Plaque sponsored by Bill & Peg Stanley
Located in the Colonial Cemetery

ONCE UPON A TIME IN NORWICH, an 18 year old Benedict Arnold stood on this spot and watched as they lowered his long-suffering mother into her grave. Benedict himself was an apprentice, bound by indentured servitude to his mother's cousins, the Lathrop Brothers. His father was suffering from alcohol-induced dementia, believed caused by sadness over losing four children: Absalom, Elizabeth, Mary, and an earlier son named Benedict, who died an infant in 1739. The children are all buried here.

Hannah Arnold died on August 15, 1759; her husband some years later. Young Benedict moved to New Haven with his sister, Hannah, and became extremely successful. He married Margaret Mansfield who died June 19, 1775. In

Benedict Arnold's grandson, Hugh Arnold (six times removed) at the Hannah Arnold Gravesite.

New Haven, Arnold founded and commanded the 2nd Connecticut Foot Guard. During the American Revolution, he was a hero and became George Washington's finest field general, winning many victories. Benedict Arnold built and commanded America's first naval fleet of 16 vessels. The crew included 30 Marines that engaged the British in America's first naval battle at Valcour Island on Lake Champlain, October 11, 1776.

After the Battle of Saratoga, October 7, 1777, British General John Burgoyne said of Arnold, "It was his victory." Then a major general, Arnold was severely wounded and crippled for life. Assigned to Philadelphia, he married Margaret Shippen from a neutralist-loyalist family. She was later awarded a lifetime pension by King George III for "Her service to the Crown in the Colonies." General Arnold, after the marriage, betrayed his young country and returned his loyalty to the Crown and planned to surrender West Point, which he later commanded, and General Washington to the British. To this day, he is America's most famous traitor.

As British brigadier, he was ordered by Commanding General Henry Clinton to rout the privateers from the Port of New London. On September 6, 1781, troops under the command of Benedict Arnold burned the City of New London. Other British troops, under the command of Lt. Colonel Edmund Eyre, attacked Fort Griswold in Groton where many lives were lost in what was described as a massacre.

Local citizens, outraged at the treasonous act, descended as a mob on this cemetery and removed the gravestones of the father, Benedict, and the infant son, Benedict.

The only epitaph that remains is to Hannah King Arnold:

IN MEMORY OF
Hannah ye well beloved
Wife of Capt. Benedict
Arnold & Daughter of
Mr. John & Elizabeth
Waterman, (She was a
Pattern of Piety Patience
And Virtue) who died
August 15, 1759
AEtatis Suae 52"

Samuel Huntington Home

Plaque sponsored by the Gernon Trust
Located on 34 East Town Street

The Samuel Huntington Home

Lawyer, judge, diplomat, and President of the Continental Congress, Samuel Huntington left an indelible mark on the history of Norwich and the United States. His life reflected the independence and ambition of a growing nation. He saw Norwich change from a colonial possession to membership within a republic larger than any nation in Europe.

A descendent of Norwich's founding fathers, Huntington was born in Scotland, Connecticut in 1731. From an early age, Huntington displayed intelligence and a desire to do more than was expected of him. While apprenticed as a cooper, he made time to teach himself Latin. This zest for learning caught the attention of Rev. Ebenezer Devotion, who urged young Samuel to continue his education, by allowing him access to his extensive library and introducing him to Eliphalet Dyer and Jedediah Elderkin. Prominent lawyers and patriots, these men shaped Huntington's future by schooling him in the law. Passing the bar exam in 1758, Huntington soon married Martha Devotion (daughter of Rev. Ebenezer), and moved to Norwich in 1760. Four short years later, he was elected as Norwich's representative to the Connecticut General Assembly. A year later, he rallied his constituents to stand firm against the dreaded Stamp Act.

Over the next twenty years Huntington's reputation for fairness and integrity grew. He was appointed superior court judge and justice of the peace. In 1775, he was named a delegate to the Continental Congress. Professional growth was matched by personal growth when he adopted three of his relative's children and raised them as his own.

The many years of dedicated service resulted in Huntington being elected President of the second Continental

Congress from 1779-1781. His service as President of the Continental Congress coincided with the ratification with the Articles of Confederation and Perpetual Union, our first Constitution, which declared that whoever is President of the Continental Congress shall serve as President of the United States.

On March 1, 1781, Maryland became the final state to ratify the Articles of Confederation, thus making Norwich's Samuel Huntington the first President of the United States in Congress Assembled. This is an undeniably true fact.

Unfortunately, due to health problems, Huntington tried to retire from public service later in 1781, but was to continue in elected public office. In 1784, he became Connecticut's Chief Justice, and in 1786, Governor of Connecticut, a post he would occupy for ten years. A testament of his popularity as Norwich's adopted son was that in his last election for governor, he received all 900 votes from Norwich's eligible voters. Huntington died on January 5, 1796 at age 64.

His home on East Town Street, built in 1783, is a reflection of a modest man who achieved greatness as Governor, Chief Justice, President of the Continental Congress and first President of the United States of America under the Articles of Confederation in Congress Assembled.

Samuel Huntington

The Glebe House
Located on 62 Church Street

The Glebe House

Built in 1768 this was the home of the Reverend John Tyler, Rector of Christ Church for 54 years. He had been ordained by the Bishop of London. During the Revolution religious services were held in the house.

Reverend Tyler took part in the historic meeting of March 25, 1783 at the Glebe House in Woodbury, Connecticut, at which Samuel Seabury was selected as the first American Episcopal Bishop. The house was later occupied by William Tyler Olcott, author and astronomer, who was the great-great-grandson of the Reverend Tyler.

Benedict Arnold

Plaque sponsored by Bruce McDermott
Located on 299 Washington Street

Benedict Arnold was born here in January 1741. He and a younger sister, Hannah, were the only children in the family of his father, also named Benedict, and his mother, Hannah Waterman King, to survive killer childhood diseases and reach adulthood.

Many tales have circulated about Arnold's wild, undisciplined childhood, but virtually none is true. His father's health problems caused young Benedict to leave school and become an apprentice to his mother's cousins, Daniel and Joshua Lathrop. Those two Norwichites taught him the apothecary's trade and then helped set him up in business in New Haven, Connecticut. There, Arnold became a prosperous merchant, heavily involved in the West Indies trade.

The Revolution Fostered Arnold's remarkable talents as a daring commander on land and water. He fought courageously at Ticonderoga, Quebec, Lake Champlain, and at the pivotal battles of Saratoga. He repelled a British force at Danbury, Connecticut for which the Continental Congress finally named him a major general. George Washington praised Arnold as his fighting general.

Original oil painting of Benedict Arnold by Doug Henry of Hanover, NH.

Wounded seriously at Quebec and then again at Saratoga, and seeing how poorly Congress supported its army, Arnold started to doubt the merits of the patriot cause. Problems with local officials in Philadelphia during 1778, after Washington named him military governor there, added to his growing disillusionment. After a vicious public attack on his character, Arnold opened negotiations with the British. He believed the Revolution had lost its way and would collapse, and he hoped to lead the people in settling their differences with the Crown short of independence.

In September 1780, amid a failed plot to turn patriot defenses at West Point, NY over to the British, Arnold defected. The British awarded him the rank of brigadier and indemnified him for his property losses, although more had been requested.

As a British officer, Arnold led attacks on Richmond, VA and in September, 1781 on New London, Connecticut. The massacre of American soldiers at Fort Griswold across the Thames River, that day, as well as the burning of New London, further increased patriotic enmity toward Arnold. He was not at Fort Griswold but was in overall command of the troops who attacked that bastion.

After the war, Arnold resumed his mercantile career, trading out of Canada and England. He never quite enjoyed the prosperity of his earlier years. Arnold died in London in June 1801, aged 60 years, his name, despite his invaluable service to the patriot cause, to become synonymous with treason.

His remains are interred at St. Mary's of Battersea Church in London with his wife, Margaret Shippen Arnold, and daughter, Sophia.

Text by Professor James Kirby Martin, author, historian, professor of history.

Captain Robert Niles Monument

Located on 37 Oak Street

The Captain Robert Niles Monument

Captain Robert Niles of Norwich was Commander of the Revolutionary War vessel, *The Spy*. He was employed by the government to carry to France an official copy of the treaty ratified with that kingdom in 1778, known as the *Treaties Of Commerce And Alliance*. Of six copies dispatched by different ships, Capt. Niles' copy was the only one able to pass through the British blockade and arrived at Brest in 21 days. This treaty hastened the departure of troops and stores which France sent to the aid of the American cause. This treaty was the result of General Benedict Arnold's victory at Saratoga on October 7, 1777; France entered the Revolutionary War actively on the American side leading to ultimate victory at Yorktown.

The inscription reads:

Capt.
ROBERT NILES
A patriot who commanded
the Spy during the Revolution.
He carried the treaty to France
delivering it to
BENJ. FRANKLIN
Capt. Niles served his country
faithfully and died a Christian
in the year 1818
aged 83 years.

Washington Crossing

Plaque sponsored by the Society of the Founders of Norwich, Connecticut
Located on 173 North Main Street (N.P.U. property)

THIS MARKS THE WAY TO
THE OLD FERRY OVER THE
SHETUCKET RIVER MAINTAINED
BY THE TOWN FROM 1671 TO 1784
AND USED BY
GEORGE WASHINGTON
MARCH 5, 1781 ON HIS WAY TO
NEWPORT, R. I.
THIS TABLET PLACED BY THE SOCIETY OF THE
FOUNDERS OF NORWICH, CONNECTICUT, 1932

Two bronze tablets set in boulders were placed on North Main Street in 1932 by the Society of the Founders of Norwich to mark the way to the old Ferry across the Shetucket River, used by George Washington.

Springtime is approaching in 1781 and so also is the beginning of the end for England's war against American independence. General Washington visits Norwich, then one of our largest cities, on his way to Newport to plan strategy with General Rochambeau, commander of 6,000 French soldiers sent by King Louis XVI. Admiral Grasse's French navy gains control of Chesapeake waters just as English General Cornwallis sets up camp at Yorktown, Virginia. Combined French and U.S. armies trap Cornwallis by land as Admiral Grasse prevents an escape by sea. General Cornwallis surrenders 8,000 English soldiers on October 17, 1781. England realizes U.S. independence is inevitable and agrees to a peace treaty signed in Paris on September 3, 1783.

Samuel Huntington Tomb

Plaque sponsored by Bill and Peg Stanley
Located in the Colonial Cemetery

The Samuel Huntington Tomb

This tomb is the final resting place of Samuel Huntington and his wife, Martha, born July 16, 1731 in what is now Scotland, Connecticut. He was self-educated and became an attorney. His first law practice was in Willimantic. He later moved to Norwich in 1861 as Norwich was more affluent.

He was a delegate from Connecticut to the Continental Congress and one of only 56 men who signed the Declaration of Independence and the Articles of Confederation. He served as President of the Continental Congress from 1779-1781 and was Justice of the Connecticut Supreme Court from 1784-1785, and Governor of Connecticut from 1786 until his death, January 5, 1796.

The tomb was found to be in disrepair in 2002, and a drive led by Bill Stanley restored the tomb at a cost of $130,000 in cash and in-kind services. It was during the restoration that it was discovered Samuel Huntington actually was the first President of the United States under our first Constitution, the Articles of Confederation which stated whoever serves as President of the Continental Congress in Congress Assembled shall also serve as President of the United States.

Samuel Huntington was President of the Continental Congress on March 1, 1781 when Maryland became the last of the 13 colonies to ratify the Articles of Confederation. Because Samuel Huntington was then President of the Continental Congress when America became a nation for the first time, he was automatically the first President of the United States under our first Constitution, the Articles of Confederation in Congress Assembled.

Chelsea Parade

Plaque sponsored by Thomas Fanning, Joseph Perkins, & Joshua Lathrop
Located at the intersection of Washington Street and Broadway

(left) Chelsea Parade plaque

(far left & top) World War II Monuments on Chelsea Parade.

"Formerly Williams Park, this unoccupied piece of ground had long been used by the military companies of the district as a place for military practice and regimental reviews.

"In 1797 the title was cleared of all incumbrances and claims by Joseph Perkins, Thomas Fanning, and Joshua Lathrop, and deeded by them to the Town of Norwich as a park or public parade forever." – Caulkins.

According to Sarah Lester Tyler, on September 11, 1792, the 20th Regiment of Infantry was reviewed on this plain and after that it was always called "The Chelsea Parade." – *Norwich Book of Deeds*

The plaque inscription reads:

CHELSEA PARADE
GIVEN TO THE
TOWN OF NORWICH
FOR THE USE AND PURPOSE OF
A PUBLIC PARADE OR OPEN WALK
BY
THOMAS FANNING
JOSEPH PERKINS
JOSHUA LATHROP
APRIL 5, 1797

Eliza Huntington Home

Located on 99 Washington Street

The Eliza Huntington House

The original owner of this land was Elijah Lathrop. In 1807 it was transferred to his grandson, John Lathrop, who may have had this house built, although there is no house mentioned in the deed.

The next owner was Jonathan Dodge who purchased the property in 1832. The use of Greek Revival ornament indicates the house was probably built for him. In 1836 Jedediah Huntington purchased the property with dwelling house and barn, and it remained in his family until the 1870s when he left it in his will as a home for aged women as a memorial to his wife, Eliza.

Lydia Huntley Sigourney School

Plaque sponsored by the Gernon Trust
Located on 189 Broadway

Born September 1, 1791 in Norwich, Ms. Sigourney was an outspoken activist, humanitarian, and consummate poet. She published approximately 50 volumes of poetry and literature, starting with her 1815 work entitled *Moral Pieces In Prose And Verse.*

Lydia's father, Ezekiel Huntley, was the gardener for Dr. Daniel Lathrop, under whose roof the Huntley's lived (Dr. Lathrop was the same individual who apprenticed Benedict Arnold, in his apothecary shop). Treated as a member of the Lathrop's extended family, Lydia was privy to the fineries of Norwich, which would have been out of her reach as a child of a servant. The East District School, which she attended, was noted for teaching both sexes in the same room and the same

The Lydia Huntley Sigourney School

subject matters. This profoundly influenced Lydia and fostered her progressive attitude towards the education of females. In 1811, she and Maria Hyde opened a school for girls (189 Broadway, facing on the little plain). The mission of the school was to teach young women all subjects and encourage them to expect more from life than being teachers themselves (a profession that women of learning were limited to at that time).

After marrying Charles Sigourney in 1819, Lydia and her school relocated to Hartford. She mingled with the upper echelon of society. She dined with U.S. Presidents and European royalty. Her poems and prose reflected her worldly experiences. Sigourney was also a philanthropist. When she started her school, a tenth (tithe) was given to charity. Her biographer (Gordon Haight, in his work *The Sweet Singer Of Hartford*), said that "the Indians, Greeks, missionaries in Asia and Africa, as well as at home, regularly received her unobtrusive gifts. The poor and sick in Hartford were constantly being supplied with clothes and provisions."

The laureate was unappreciated and ignored in her native Norwich. In Caulkins' *History Of Norwich*, Sigourney is described as one who has "acquired a literary fame second to that of no female in the country." Hartford named a street for her. *The Hartford Courant's* obituary labeled her writings as, "models of pure and elegant English . . . contributing to educate the national taste, and instruct the literary judgement of our people, by the purity and simplicity of her rhetoric, as much as she has elevated and ennobled their sentiments by the deeply religious tone, which pervades all her writings." Her final book, *Letters Of Life*, was published in 1865, shortly after her death.

Captain Samuel Chester Reid

Plaque sponsored by the Eastern Connecticut Council Boy Scouts
of America & Samuel Chester Reid Memorial Association
Located on Chelsea Parade "North" next to Horse water trough

The Captain Samuel Chester Reid Monument

In memory of Captain Samuel Chester Reid (1783-1861), born at Norwich, Connecticut August 25, 1783. During the War of 1812 Commander of the American Privateer General Armstrong. Captain Reid planned the United States flag which was adopted by Congress in 1818 providing for thirteen permanent stripes and for the stars increasing with the admission of new states.

The Captain Samuel Chester Reid Monument was erected by the Eastern Connecticut Council Boy Scouts of America and Samuel Chester Reid Memorial Association during George Washington Bicentenary, 1932.

Norwich Harbor

Plaque sponsored by the Norwich Rotary
Located on Chelsea Harbor Drive

A view of Norwich Harbor with Mayor Osgood's yacht at anchor.

War with England led to a strict enforced British blockade of Thames River shipping from May 1813 to March 1815. American frigates *United States* and *Macedonian* along with sloop-of-war *Hornet* were trapped at Gales Ferry and Bushnell Cove next to Norwich in Thamesville. Dismantled ships crowded the Chelsea harbor, and with valuable mills here there was local fear of invasion as at Stonington in August, 1814, so militia stood ready.

   After peace the busy harbor thrived and on October 15, 1816 the first steamboat to dock here, *Connecticut*, created huge local interest, and on July 1, 1817 a Norwich built steamboat named *Eagle* with 50 passengers exploded during the maiden voyage on the Thames River in full view of President James Monroe on tour aboard the steamboat *Fulton*. While the embarrassment was devastating thankfully injuries to crew and passengers was minimal.

Daughters of the American Revolution

Located on 42 (Backus House) & 44 (Rockwell House) Rockwell Street

The Backus House

The Rockwell House

The Backus House (left) stood for 200 years on lower Broadway, where it was rescued from destruction by the Faith Trumbull Chapter of the Daughters of the American Revolution in 1951. Built by Nethaniel Backus in 1750, this lovely home still retains some of its original features, such as the heavy front door framed with carved rosettes and pillars.

Nethaniel Backus was a descendant of two of the founders of the town, William Backus and William Backus, Jr. Nethaniel was born on April 5, 1704. In 1726 he married Hannah Baldwin and they had several children. According to record, Nethaniel Backus was one of the six men in Norwich who owned their own carriages prior to the Revolutionary War.

Today the Backus House is open to the public as an historical monument.

Built in 1818 of granite quarried on the property, by Major Joseph Perkins, soldier and physician, the Rockwell House (right) is of special interest because of the historical items on display. Dr. John A. Rockwell, a physician, lived here for many years. He was a grandson of Major Perkins and it is for him that the house is named.

To preserve the house, his daughter, Mrs. Rockwell Cole, deeded the property to the Faith Trumbull Chapter, D. A. R., and it is now maintained as a museum by that organization.

John Fox Slater Home
(Elks Club)
Located on 352 Main Street

The John Fox Slater House – Elks Club

An early owner of this 1827 Greek Revival home was John Fox Slater, who was born in Rhode Island March 4, 1815. He was President of the Slater Cotton Mills at Jewett City, and founder of the John F. Slater Fund ($1,000,000) for the education of Negro freedmen following the Civil War, for which he was presented a gold medal by the Congress of the United States. He was also a benefactor of the Park Congregational Church, The United Workers, and Norwich Free Academy. The Slater Memorial Museum was built in honor of Mr. Slater through a bequest of his son, William A. Slater. He died in Norwich in 1884. This brick house is one of the largest examples of Greek Revival architecture in the area.

Norwich Railroad Station
Plaque sponsored by the Norwich and Worcester Railroad
Located on Railroad Avenue

(left) The freight terminal and (right) the passenger terminal of the Norwich and Worcester Railroad.

With four daily passenger and freight connections each way to Worcester, Norwich became a major transportation center with steamboat shipping to New York City through Long Island Sound. In fact the preferred Boston to New York route was via the Norwich and Worcester Railroad through Norwich!

Until the Thames River was bridged in 1889, Chelsea Harbor had full warehouse and passenger terminals with its favorable access to central New England. There was also a large steam engine and car manufacturing factory on North Main Street that supplied rolling stock to all U.S. railroads.

While the Norwich and Worcester Railroad operated on 59 miles of track ending along the east bank of the Thames River, eventually extending to Groton, a second railroad called New London, Willimantic, and Palmer (Massachusetts) operated along the west bank with a station on Hollyhock Island. That company became New London Northern and then Central Vermont Railroad. A connector track laid in 1854 along Chelsea Harbor joined the Norwich and Worcester Railroad with this second railroad.

In addition to the trains, electric trolley cars also used the tracks between 1880 to 1924 with eight trips daily each way between Norwich and Worcester.

A sill from the Norwich and Worcester Railroad freight house built in 1839 and destroyed by hurricane, September 21, 1938, reads:

NORWICH AND WORCESTER
RAILROAD
OPENED MARCH 9, 1840
LEASED TO BOSTON, HARTFORD, ERIE R.R. . . . 1869
LEASED TO NEW YORK, NEW ENGLAND R.R. . . . 1886
LEASED TO NEW ENGLAND R.R. . . . 1896
LEASED TO N.Y., N.H., H. R.R. . . . 1898
CENTENIAL EXERCISES SPONSORED BY THE
NEW LONDON RAILROAD ASSOCIATION

Yantic Cemetery

Located on Lafayette Street

Yantic Cemetery

Yantic Cemetery is not located in the village of Yantic. It is situated on 26.05 acres along Lafayette Street in Norwich and is named for the Yantic River which curves around and cuts the western border along a steep embankment.

The cemetery was planned in Victorian fashion in a park-like setting that was intended to be more comforting than prior stark burial grounds. It was also a necessary addition to the fast growing Noriwich population as Oak Street Cemetery was nearing capacity.

So it was that on July 12, 1844, the cemetery was consecrated with all denominations of Christians uniting in the service. Dr. Bond of Second Congregational Church gave the address with a prayer by Episcopal Rector Mr. Paddock.

It is the resting place of so many Norwich "giants" of the 19th century with magnificent monuments; also within it's grounds are the final graves of Civil War soldiers who died at the infamous Andersonville, Georgia P.O.W. camp. Seven are reinterred in a Circle of Honor. Many other Civil War soldiers and sailors are buried here along with five Norwich generals and one admiral.

Yantic Cemetery is very well maintained by the City Public Works Department, and "Guns of Norwich" members annually decorate graves of veterans with a flag.

Norwich Free Academy

Located on 305 Broadway

The campus at NFA in its spring splendor.

Incorporated in 1854, the Norwich Free Academy opened its doors in 1856 with a student body of 80 and a faculty of three teachers. An endowed academy, the school was the project of a group of wealthy, civic minded individuals led by Reverend John Putnam Gulliver, who at the urging of another city politician and businessman, John Breed, set out to found a school for the community's youth of both genders. The first graduating class consisted of two young men in 1856.

The original 11 room Academy, a building of Italianate architectural design, stood on the site of the present Tirrell Building until 1909 when it was razed and the new structure erected. By that time, the campus had grown to include the Slater Memorial Building (1886), the Manual Training Building (1895), and the Converse Building (1906). Today, the Norwich Free Academy consists of nine academic buildings on a 38-acre campus. The latest addition is the Sydney E. Frank Center for Visual and Performing Arts (2005) in the southeast corner of the campus.

Slater Memorial Museum is one of two professional museums on a secondary school campus, nationally, and its relationship with the Academy, represents the American Victorian Athenaeum model, a unique institutional relationship to share the cultural mission of furthering education, displaying fine arts, preserving history, and fostering study of literature and natural sciences. The founding of the Norwich Art School in 1890 forms a third institutional relationship, and the longevity of this triad attests to the Academy's national significance. In 155 years of existence, the Academy has been led by only eleven Heads of School, consistent stewardship and care that account for the school's sustainability. An active, involved, and generous alumni community of over 35,000 supports their alma mater, and the Academy's alumni reach is global.

Originally a "restricted" school, the Academy required students to pass rigorous entrance examinations. In time, the school dropped entrance requirements and became the designated high school serving the city of Norwich and seven surrounding communities (Bozrah, Canterbury, Franklin, Lisbon, Preston, Sprague, and Voluntown), as well as tuition students. It still retains its original independent governance by a private, self-perpetuating Board of Trustees.

Today, the Norwich Free Academy, the home of the Wildcats, the largest high school in the state of Connecticut, offers a unique combination of private and public education to a student population of approximately 2,600 students. It is a diverse population – geographically, ethnically, linguistically, and socio-economically – unparalleled in diversity. Since 1854, in the words of founder Rev. John P. Gulliver at the 1856 dedication ceremony, the mission of the Norwich Free Academy has been to "return to our hamlets and our homes its priceless freight of youthful minds, enriched by learning, developed by a liberal culture, refined by study of all that is beautiful in nature and art, and prepared for the highest usefulness and the purest happiness."

Slater Museum

Plaque sponsored by Gorin's Furniture
Located on 305 Broadway

Samuel Slater, possessing considerable knowledge of textile production and machinery, emigrated from England in 1789. He was attracted by the United States because of the bounty offered here for skilled textile workers. British law prohibited people, like Slater, from exporting drawings of relevant manufacturing equipment and their operation or selling it to competitors. Upon his arrival to America Slater constructed versions of the Arkwright spinning and carding machines, which he used in establishing the U.S. cotton textile industry in Pawtucket, Rhode Island in 1793.

A descendent, John Fox Slater, was prominent in the local textile industry and president of the huge Ponemah Mill complex, which still exists today in the Taftville section of Norwich. In 1882, he donated, the then extraordinary sum of one million dollars, to educate "freed slaves" in the south. Eventually, 36 colleges were recipients of these funds. Slater was awarded the Congressional Medal of Honor for this act.

The attractive Romanesque styled Slater Museum (designed by Stephen Earle) was a gift by his son, William Slater, to the Norwich Free Academy in memory of his father. It was dedicated November 4, 1886. The extensive collection of Greek, Roman, and Renaissance casts is considered the finest in the country. Included are such masterpieces as Michelangelo's Pieta and the Greek, Venus De Milo.

Opposite the museum is Chelsea Parade. This area was once planted with Indian Corn and later used as a training ground for the local militia.

The Slater Museum

Buckingham Memorial

Plaque sponsored by Chelsea-Groton Savings Bank
Located on 307 Main Street

Once upon a time in Norwich, the Governor of the State of Connecticut, William A. Buckingham, resided in this building. Born in Lebanon, Connecticut, May 28, 1804, he attended Lebanon School, Bacon Academy in Colchester, and later took up residency in Norwich.

Impressed by his uncle's retail establishment, young Buckingham first went into retailing and later invested in the manufacture of carpets and the rubber shoe industry. Successful in all of these enterprises, he amassed a fortune and was able to dedicate his life thereafter to public service.

He became Mayor of Norwich in 1847; elected Governor of the State of Connecticut in 1858. He was a loyal

Governor Buckingham's residence.

friend to candidate, and later President, Abraham Lincoln. Buckingham served Connecticut as Governor during the Civil War. After Lincoln's assassination, Buckingham resigned his office in 1866. He was elected in May, 1868 to fill the first vacancy which occurred in the Senate of the United States. His remarkable career was an inspiration to all. He met the demand of every public occasion. Buckingham was a man of honor with strong religious commitments. Sympathetic and charitable, he was considered a statesman.

He died while in office on February 5, 1875. His funeral was attended by numerous national dignitaries.

His residence, this building, is dedicated as a memorial to the memory of William A. Buckingham – Mayor of Norwich, Governor of Connecticut, and United States Senator.

———————

William Buckingham, Connecticut Civil War Governor, supported the war effort 100% and was a very active an patriotic governor. Governor Buckingham was watching every movement the South was making to continue slavery into the Western territories and felt war was imminent and that Connecticut should be ready.

On January 17, 1861, he issued a proclamation stating the traitorous and hostile acts of the South. With clear vision and resolute purpose, he declared that the active services of the militia may soon be required and urged companies to fill their ranks and inspect their arms and equipment. On his own responsibility, he quietly ordered his Quartermaster General to purchase the latest arms and equipment for 5,000 men.

When Connecticut's first three infantry regiments reached Washington, D.C. the General of the Army, Winfield Scott, commented that the Connecticut regiments were the best equipped.

Approximately 1300 Norwich men served during the Civil War, 1216 in the Army and 84 in the Navy. 156 did not return alive. They served in 21 of 29 regiments, 2 heavy artillery regiments, 1 light battery, 1 cavalry regiment and U.S. Naval ships. Several served in other states' regiments. They fought in 33 battles or engagements. Many were present at Appomattex, VA when Robert E. Lee surrendered to General Ulysses S. Grant.

Brigadier General Daniel Tyler of Norwich was selected by Lt. General Winfield Scott, commander of the U.S. Army to lead the Northern Advance with his division. They met the Confederate Army on July 18, 1861. The first major battle of the Civil War, known as Bull Run by the Northerners and Manassas by the Southerners.

Lafayette Foster Home

Located on 315 Broadway

The house of Lafayette Foster, currently the Edwin H. Land Library and Norton-Peck Reading Room.

Today Lafayette Foster's home serves as the Edwin H. Land Library and is known as The Norton-Peck Reading Room in honor of Henry B. Norton who left a bequest to establish a library. This was combined with the previously established Peck Library, the gift of Harriet Peck Williams in memory of her father, Capt. Bela Peck. The Norwich Board of Trade included Lafayette Foster on their 1865 list as one of the wealthiest men in Norwich.

Lafayette Foster Gravesite

Located in Yantic Cemetery

The Lafayette Foster Gravesite
(top-left) Lafayette Foster

Lafayette Foster was born in Franklin, Connecticut in November 1806. Following graduation from Brown University he became a lawyer practicing in Norwich for more than 30 years. He was elected mayor of Norwich in 1835 and 1852. He represented this city in the General Assembly for six terms and was elected speaker of the Connecticut House of Representatives for three of those terms. Foster later became United States Senator, serving for eleven years. On March 6, 1865 the 39th Congress, elected Lafayette Foster President pro-tem of the U.S. Senate. Six weeks later, following the assassination of Abraham Lincoln, Andrew Johnson, the Vice President, advanced to become the new President and Lafayette Foster moved up to become the Vice President of the United States (April 15, 1865). A position he held for almost two years. He ran for reelection but was defeated. In 1870 Foster was elected to the Supreme Court of Connecticut, serving six years until he retired due to the age limit rule. He then returned to Norwich where he continued his prestigious and successful law practice.

   Foster married Joanna Boylston Lanman in October 1837. They had three children, all of whom died in early childhood. Joanna died in 1859. Foster remarried in 1860 to Martha Prince Lyman. The couple had no children. Lafayette Foster died of malarial fever in 1880.

Otis Library

Plaque sponsored by the Otis Library
Located on Union Square

Pencil drawing of original Otis Library.

Once upon a time in Norwich . . . Joseph Otis, who had earned his fortune elsewhere, returned to his hometown at the age of 70, and wishing to do something lasting for the people of Norwich, founded a public library in his name on this spot. He purchased the land and planned to have the library built after his death, but at the urging of his pastor, he completed construction of the building during his lifetime.

Opening in 1850, under the administration of Otis' handpicked Board of Trustees, Otis Library served the city at this location until it relocated to Main Street in 1962.

Daniel Tyler

In the early moments of the Civil War, Governor Buckingham relied greatly on Norwich resident, at 130 Washington Street, Captain Daniel Tyler (age 62), a graduate of West Point and having served in the U.S. Army for approximately 15 years, was familiar with the details of military organization.

On April 18, 1861 Captain Tyler was promoted to Colonel and Commanding Officer of the Connecticut 1st Infantry Regiment. On April 22, 1861 the companies of the Regiment (located throughout the state) were ordered to move to New Haven to begin training. Since Tyler was the only professional soldier in the Regiment, he had a huge responsibility placed upon him to train such a large amount of raw troops.

Soon after reaching Washington, D.C. with his Regiment, Daniel Tyler was promoted to Brigadier General at the earnest request of the Commander in Chief of the U.S. Army, Lt. General Winfield Scott. So impressed with the 39,000 troops that had assembled, General Scott was heard to remark that the Connecticut troops were the best disciplined, best equipped, and best trained.

Brigadier General Daniel Tyler

President Lincoln was well aware his forces were not yet prepared for a major battle but found it hard to resist the call of the press and public. More importantly, he had learned that a large Confederate Army was moving north from Richmond, Virginia and could pose a threat to Washington. President Lincoln ordered Lt. General Scott to use his 39,000-man army to stop the northern advance.

General Tyler then was ordered to lead the federal advance with his Infantry Division. They met the Confederate Army on July 18, 1861 at Manassas, Virginia. The battle is known as Bull Run by the North and Manassas by the South. The battle was won by the Confederate Army.

General Tyler returned to the state and rendered great service to the state and country in seeing the new forming Connecticut Regiments 14 through 21 were prepared for the field.

Again in March 1862, General Tyler returned to federal service and was assigned to command a brigade then a division in the Army of Mississippi.

General Tyler's civilian profession was civil engineer. He founded the city of Anniston, Alabama and was buried there in early December 1882 at age 83.

The 26ᵗʰ Regiment

Plaque sponsored by the Waitte Insurance Agency
Located on Union Street at Broadway

The monument commemorating the Battle of Port Hudson and the 26th Regiment.

Once upon a time in Norwich, the 26th Regiment Connecticut Volunteers formed. The members were all from Eastern Connecticut. During the Civil War, 194 of them were killed or wounded in one day. This monument is to their memory.

There is no single event in the history of Eastern Connecticut that was more tragic than the Battle of Fort Hudson fought on May 27, 1863.

Port Hudson was strategic to the Confederate strategy and was the backdoor for providing supplies and ammunition. The great ports of Charleston, South Carolina and Savannah, Georgia were blockaded. It was a time prior to the Battle of Gettysburg and Vicksburg.

There were 557 men in the 26th Regiment, and on that single day, in the heat of the state of Louisiana, on the banks of the Mississippi, 52 were killed and 142 wounded. The casualty rate was 30%; worse than the Battle of Iwo Jima or the Invasion of Normandy during World War II.

Andersonville Circle of Honor

Plaque sponsored by Harrison C. Noyes
Located in Yantic Cemetery

Their bodies were returned to Norwich and buried in a circle where the American flag flies day and night.

Once upon a time in Norwich, nine victims of the Civil War were reinterred in this circle. Their stones are marked Andersonville. France's Devil's Island and the infamous Bataan Death March were parallel in horrors to Andersonville where they died during the Civil War.

Andersonville, Georgia was a prison camp; the cruelest prison camp in all American history. During the winter of 1864, and the following three months of 1865, 13,000 Union soldiers died. Of that number, 15 were from Norwich.

The prison was but a few acres in which 41,000 men were packed. They were provided no shelter, only a handful of meal mush a day, and a polluted stream was their water supply. There were absolutely no sanitary facilities whatever. The clothing they wore was salvaged from their dead comrades. The temperature in the winter of 1864-5 fell to almost zero. The summer heat reached 110°. They tortured the men. They murdered them. They died of exposure and starvation. These crimes on Americans were committed by Americans. An average of 3,000 died each month; 100 a day. Some were shot by guards for no other reason than they wandered too close to the fence.

When the war was over, the City of Norwich sent George W. Smith to Andersonville to bring back the bodies of Norwich's men and boys to be reinterred at this site. There were 30 Norwich men prisoners. Fifteen of them died. Only ten bodies could be identified. Nine of them are buried here, in Yantic Cemetery. George W. Ward is buried in the family plot at the City Cemetery, and his stone is marked Andersonville. Seven of the nine are buried here together in this circle, and are memorialized by the Civil War cannon and the American flag that flies day and night in their honor.

Ponemah Mill

Plaque sponsored by the Gernon Trust
Located on Route 69 & Route 97, Taftville

Aerial view of Taftville with Ponemah Mills in foreground. Taftville circa 1940.
1. No. 1 Mill; 2. No. 2 Mill; 3. No.3 Mill; 4. Maintenance Departments; 5. Canal and Water Wheel; 6. Boarding House; 7. Company Store and Ponemah Hall; 8. Congregational Church; 9. Providence St.; 10. South A St.; 11. South B St.; 12. South C St. 13. North A St.; 14. North B St.; 15. Second Ave. a.k.a. Front St.; 16. Third Ave.; 17. Slater Ave.; (foremen's residences); 18. Superintendent's Mansion; 19. Wequonnoc School; 20. Sacred Heart Church; 21. Sacred Heart School; 22. Dugas Studio; (Est. 1882, contains a photographic history of Taftville) 23. SHYMA-SHYLA Club; (site of first Sacred Heart Church); 24. Site of first Sacred Heart School (Nun's Residence is still evident.); 25 Caron Residence on a high ledge; 26. Providence Street "Ball Ground"; 27. Site of "Balancing Rock"; 28. Cow Barn; 29. Horse Barn; 30. Site of Prentice Roller Shop; Below; The Number 4 Weave Shop; (built 1910, was the largest building in Norwich, 700 feet long and 200 feet wide.)

Construction of the great Ponemah Cotton Mill began in 1866. A group of investors, led by Edward and Cyrus Taft of Providence, Rhode Island, purchased a 600 acre farm on the Shetucket River. The first mill was 750 feet long and 74 feet wide. It began operation in 1871. The name "Ponemah" was taken from Longfellow's poem, Song of Hiawatha, and was said to mean "our hope." The mill owners built a village to house the workers, naming it Taftville after the principal investors. The main street of the new village was named Providence Street.

The Ponemah Mill spun and wove imported Egyptian cotton into very high quality cloth for the luxury trade. A bitter strike in 1875, led to the eviction of mill workers who were mostly comprised of Irish Americans. New workers were recruited from French Canada. Taftville became noted as a French Canadian community.

Major expansions of the mill were made in 1884, 1902, and 1910. At its peak, the Ponemah Mill employed 1600 workers and produced over 20 million yards of cloth a year. They boasted that a pound of cotton could be spun into a single strand of yarn 100 miles long. In the 20th century, the mill successfully converted to the production of synthetic fabrics. It closed in 1972; one of the last great New England mills to shut down. Today, a variety of stereophonic equipment, woolen yarn spinning, and automated production control equipment, as well as a number of retail shops, occupies its space.

Norwich Grange Hall

Plaque sponsored by the Norwich Grange
Located on West Town Street at Route 395

The West Town Street School that later served as the Norwich Grange Hall.

West Town Street District School, 1869. The Bean Hill Academy, a private school, was established here in 1782. It occupied the former Separatist Church. Jedediah Morse, the "father of American geography," author of a widely used geography text, was a teacher. Early Methodist meetings were held in the building. The academy closed after 30 years. The first floor was then used for a public school, the second floor for Methodist meetings until 1831.

The old academy was eventually demolished, and replaced with a smaller public school. By the 1860's, the new building no longer met the needs of the growing school population, as new immigrants moved in to work in the mills. A protracted battle ensued between the "old stock" Yankees and the local residents and immigrants who recognized the need for change. In 1869, the new West Town Street School, the present building, was built providing adequate facilities for local needs.

In 1926 a new school, the Samuel Huntington School, was authorized. After completion, the old West Town Street School was sold to the Norwich Grange which has occupied it ever since, holding regular meetings, fairs, and making the facility available for public use.

This plaque is dedicated in memory of all departed Norwich Grange members.

Norwich City Hall

Plaque sponsored by the City of Norwich
Located on Union Square

Norwich City Hall

In colonial times, the court and town hall was located on the Norwichtown Green but in 1829 was moved to Court Street on Jail Hill in Chelsea – a gesture commensurate with the economic and political influence gained by the harbor district. Fire destroyed that building in 1865, and the current imposing Second Empire structure was constructed between 1870-1873.

This combined county courthouse and city hall office building, inspired by the Louvre, with an impressive facade of Philadelphia pressed brick and window trimmed granite, is located prominently on Union Square. Total cost of $324,732 was enormous and illustrated Norwich's prestige and wealth.

Local construction firms involved designer and general contractor, Burdick and Arnold, with another local contractor, John Murphy, laying the foundation. Joseph Smith installed the brick and granite.

Following 127 years of use and service, a total of $4,500,000 was expended in the year 2000 on maintenance code renovations.

The Alms Fire

Plaque sponsored by the Norwich Grange
Located on Asylum Street

The site of the poor farm and the mental asylum that was destroyed by fire.

Once upon a time in Norwich, behind this site, stood the poor farm and the mental asylum for which Asylum Street was named. Norwich's first poor house was on lower Washington Street. As the city prospered, successful merchants, bankers, manufacturers and sea captains built mansions on Washington Street, forcing the poor farm to this site.

One March 12, 1876, at 2:00 a.m., a fire was reported. The facility, having been deliberately removed to this remote section of town, burned before help arrived. Sixteen mental patients, locked in their rooms, were unable to escape and burned to death. In this field, most of those bodies are buried.

The poor farm was rebuilt and used for many years. Those who died there without friends or family, numbering well over 100, are also buried beneath this field in unmarked graves. In later years, mental patients were cared for at the Norwich State Hospital. The poor farm was ultimately abandoned, sold and was again destroyed by fire in 1956.

Hopkins & Allen

**Plaque sponsored by David and Karen Warfield
in honor of Edward J. Rogalski
Located on Chestnut Street at Willow Street**

The ruins of Norwich's biggest employer, Hopkins & Allen Gun Factory.

Once upon a time in Norwich, Hopkins & Allen Gun Factory was the city's largest employer. During the Civil War, Norwich provided more arms for the Union forces than any other city. As the nation's largest armory, Hopkins & Allen was just one of many gun factories in Norwich.

It was a cold February 4, 1900 when the four-story brick building on this site caught fire. It was February, and so at six in the morning it was dark, and the streets were lighted by gas lamps. The fire was discovered by the night watchman, Joe Skelly. By the time the fire department arrived, it was too late to save the building, and Hopkins & Allen was destroyed in the biggest fire in the history of Norwich. It imposed a special hardship, for all of the gunsmiths' tools were lost in the flames. Without those tools, the entire work force was unemployed.

A new 80,000 square foot Hopkins & Allen was built on the same site and rededicated in March of 1901. The 220 foot long, 60 foot wide, four-story building cost approximately $55,000.

Hopkins & Allen Arms Company, which began operations in 1868, continued in business until 1917. The World War I Armistice was given as the reason for going out of business.

Backus Hospital

Plaque sponsored by Backus Hospital
Located on 326 Washington Street

Backus Hospital

Norwich was founded in 1659, but more than two centuries passed before the city had a hospital. On October 4, 1893 – with a grand ceremony and hundreds of delighted guests – The William W. Backus Hospital opened its doors. Ever since, our hospital has been living out its mission to improve the health of the community.

The hospital's creation was the vision of two men, icons of the Victorian era: William Albert Slater, an industrialist who served as the hospital's first president, and William Wolcott Backus, a gentleman farmer who was its first benefactor.

Today, the hospital continues its proud tradition of progress by providing care for 11,000 inpatients a year, and more than 400,000 outpatients. Backus is the "medical home" for nearly a quarter million residents of eastern Connecticut. Nearly 2,500 people work there – employees, physicians, and volunteers.

In 2008, Backus Hospital's Cancer Center received the American College of Surgeons Commission on Cancer's Outstanding Achievement Award, placing it among an elite group of cancer centers nationwide.

Backus Hospital operates the state's only trauma center east of the Connecticut River, and it is the only regional facility that has a helipad and support facility for LIFE STAR, Hartford Hospital's air ambulance helicopter.

The hospital has expanded far beyond its original building. It operates outpatient centers in Colchester, Montville, and Gales Ferry; and the 57,000-square-foot Backus Outpatient Care Center in Norwich.

Maplewood Cemetery

Plaque sponsored by the Maplewood Cemetery Board of Directors, 2002
Located on 184 Salem Turnpike

Maplewood Cemetery

Once upon a time in Norwich…the citizens realized at the turn of the century that the expansion of Yantic Cemetery, located on Lafayette Street and founded in 1843, or the City Cemetery, located on Oak Street and founded in 1755, was impractical. For this reason it was now time to locate a suitable property for a new interdenominational burial ground.

The Norwich Cemetery Association was formed on March 24, 1902, and the Osgood Farm, located in East Great Plains, was purchased on June 17, 1902. The Beebe family cemetery, which predates Maplewood by many years, is located within its boundaries.

A contest, sponsored by **The Norwich Bulletin**, offered a ten-dollar prize "to the person who should first send to **The Norwich Bulletin** the successful name for the new cemetery." Mary F. Griswold of West Main Street was the prize winner.

Upon its origin, it was decided that the new cemetery would maintain a park-like atmosphere, which was popular among modern cemeteries of that period. A variety of plantings, including shade trees, would be established to provide a comfortable setting for visitors.

Today, the 138-acre property continues to maintain a park-like atmosphere as it serves Norwich and the surrounding communities. Maplewood Cemetery is a not-for-profit, nondenominational cemetery governed by a board of directors and trustees who volunteer their time to direct the affairs of the cemetery.

Dr. Ier Manwaring Home

Located on Manwaring Road

Dr. Ier J. Manwaring and the Manwaring House.

Dr. Ier J. Manwaring was one of Norwich's first woman medical doctors. She died at the age of eighty-five in 1957. Born in Montville, Connecticut, December 29, 1872, she was the daughter of John and Mercy (Raymond) Manwaring. Her parents moved to Norwich in 1877, taking up residence in the beautiful country estate in East Great Plain where she lived until her death.

She was educated in the Broadway School (now gone) and received her medical education in Women's Medical College in Philadelphia, Pennsylvania, from which she graduated in 1895.

In World War I, as a member of the American Women's Hospital Unit No. 1, she was decorated by the French Government for service at Chateau Thierry and Belleau Wood.

Several years ago the house was moved from its original site (where the Thames Valley Institute now stands) to Manwaring Road.

Mohegan Park

Plaque sponsored by the Mohegan Tribe
Located on Judd Road off Rockwell Street

1994 Mohegan Heritage Sculpture

DONORS OF LAND
FOR
MOHEGAN PARK
1807 — 1934

LEONARD W. BACON
ALBERT S. BARD
CHARLES BARD
EDITH M. BLISS
FANNIE L. BLISS
HENRY R. BOND
MARY P. BOND
HENRY R. BOND JR.
HARRIET W. BOND TYLER
RUTH H. BOND THORNE
CHARLES P. BUSHNELL
NATHAN S. BUSHNELL
EDWARD HARLAND
MARY W. REYNOLDS
JOHN A. ROCKWELL
J. HUNT SMITH
CHARLES SPALDING ESTATE

Mohegan Park, close to the center of Norwich, has 380 acres of woods and bushes, and gardens, including a Memorial Rose Garden dedicated to all war veterans. It has 1½ miles of pathways and footpaths, and access to fishing and swimming. Many of the trees and plants within the park are the descendents of those growing when the settlers purchased Norwich from Uncas and the Mohegans. As you look around you in the heart of the park, try to imagine being here in 1659.

The Old Spring Fountain

Plaque sponsored by the East Side Fountain/Reunion Committee
Located at East Main Street & Tallman Street

The Old Spring Fountain

The "Old Spring" fountain is dedicated to the "East Side" families and friends whose contributions mad possible the restoration and relocation of this neighborhood landmark. The inscription reads:

September 23, 2001
MEMBERS OF THE EAST SIDE
FOUNTAIN/REUNION COMMITTEE
NORWICH, CONN.

William Berry	Gertrude Galligan
Gloria B. Barber	Frank J. Jacaruso, Jr.
Robert Boyd	Benjamin Lathrop
Betty Catlow	Edward Martin
Douglas Demicco	Joseph Pedace
Patricia Demicco	Matilda Pysyk
	Santo Rizzuto

Frank Demicco – Chairman
Manuel Cardoza, Jr. – Co-Chairman

East Great Plains Fire Company

Plaque sponsored by the East Great Plains Fire Company
Located on New London Turnpike at West Main Street

East Great Plains Volunteer Fire Company

East Great Plains Volunteer Fire Company was established in 1943 and is a sister station to Occum, which was also certified in 1943. The first firehouse on this site was nothing more than a shed that stood by a big tree next to a two-room schoolhouse that is now a memory and a parking lot.

The first piece of fire equipment was a pump on a small, two-wheel trailer. The first volunteer at the firehouse would hook up the trailer to the back of his car, and that constituted the only equipment we had in East Great Plains.

East Great Plains' first fire chief, Richard G. Raymond, gave his life fighting a fire at the Trading Cove. Thankfully, Chief Raymond has been the only member who has died fighting a fire, but there have been many good men who followed him as chief.

Today, East Great Plains is a proud, fully-equipped, volunteer fire company whose members dedicated their services to the City of Norwich without charge.

Norwich Memorial Rose Garden

Plaque sponsored by the Norwich Rotary
Located on Judd Road at Rockwell Street

Located on Judd Road off Rockwell Street, this signature place of our Rose City is within the boundaries of Mohegan Park. The garden covers two acres of grassy paths among 1,000+ rose bushes in 120 varieties that bloom from early June into September. It is one of 140 gardens in the U.S. that displays award winning roses in cooperation with the All American Rose Selection Inc. and was itself a 1991 Award Winner.

Better Homes & Gardens Magazine chose this site in 1949 as 1st place winner for cities 10,000-100,000 population in the "More Beautiful America" competition.

Originator of the concept and planting of the Rose Garden was Roy D. Judd with assistance from neighbor Thure Dahl during and after World War II. The garden was officially dedicated on July 11, 1949 as a memorial to those who gave their lives and those who served in World War II. A decorative surrounding 8' fence was erected in 2008 at a cost of $75,000 to prevent deer intrusion. With free admission it is estimated that 10,000 visitors annually view this beautiful attraction that is maintained to highest standards by Norwich Public Works Department.

Norwich Memorial Rose Garden

Spaulding Pond Dam

Plaque sponsored by the City of Norwich
Located at Mohegan Park Lake

(right) An aerial photo of the path of destruction. The Lake Street Playground (center) with the ruins of the Turner-Stanton Mill.

(top) Erosion created a cavernous landscape on Lake Street.

Several days of rain raised the level of Mohegan Park Pond causing concern by local city officials as to the safety of the earthen dam there. Suddenly around 9 PM a trickle of leaking waters became a deluge and a tidal wave burst through the dam and following an old stream pathway leveled everything in its way.

As the flood came down through the Lake Street area it flooded and collapsed Turner-Stanton Mill taking five employee lives. Then onto Franklin Street with an additional fatality, sweeping through Lamperell Motors and down to Franklin Square.

The monument inscription reads:

> In memoriam. This monument is dedicated to those who lost their lives to the sudden flood caused by the collapse of the Spaulding Pond Dam March 6, 1963: Madlyn Atterbury, Anna Barrett, Margaret "Honey" Moody, Alexander Pobol, Mae Robidou, and Helen Roode.

Van Tassel Explosion

Plaque sponsored by the City of Norwich
Located at Central Headquarters on West Main Street

(left) Fire Lt. Thomas LaFreniere, having survived the explosion, heads back into the blaze to help his buddies. Police Sgt. John Sisco pursues LaFreniere who is suffering shock.
(right) Van Tassel Explosion Monument

In 1962, a terrible explosion took the lives of four uniformed Norwich firemen. It was the worst loss of lives in the history of Connecticut among firemen at a single fire.

Today, at Central Fire Headquarters, there is a monument to the memory of Captain William J. Sheridan, Fireman Carl J. Burke, Fireman Leonard M. Counihan and Fireman Edward Romano who gave their lives in the performance of their duties at the Van Tassell Warehouse fire on April 3, 1962.

A historic photo of the event, taken by Bob Dick, then photographer for "The Norwich Bulletin," shows Fireman Thomas LaFreniere, who survived the explosion, heading back into the fire to rescue his buddies. He was suffering severe shock, and Police Sgt. John Sisco was able to overtake LaFreniere and escort him to safety.

"Red" McKeon Park

Located on Taftville Occum Road (Route 97) at Bridge Street

The Occum Mill site now home to R. "Red" McKeon Occum Park.

Located in the center of the Occum section of Norwich is the Robert "Red" McKeon Park filling a much appreciated need for a passive and active recreation area. This well-manicured landscape stands on the former site of Roto Print Textile Factory which burned to the ground in 1985. With substantial pollution cleanup and debris removal costs of $2,775,000 this facility officially opened in 2004 due to persistent efforts of council person John P. Mereen.

"Red" McKeon's name is synonymous with Occum where he served as fire chief from 1960-94 and founded the ambulance company in 1970; he was an advocate for securing funding and testifying before the state legislature in support of this project.

Angelo Sanquedolce
Memorial Plaza

Plaque sponsored by the City of Norwich
Located in City Hall Plaza on Union Square

THE ANGELO SANQUEDOLCE MEMORIAL PLAZA

DEDICATED MAY 14, 1999

The Heritage Riverfront Park Plaza is hereby named and dedicated in honor of Angelo J. Sanquedolce, Comptroller of the City of Norwich from 1968 to 1998, for thirty years of exemplary public service, and for numerous and lasting contributions to the well-being of others, pursuant to a resolution adopted by the Norwich City Council on November 16, 1998. His professional and personal accomplishments, expertise and commitment to excellence established a lofty standard for all to emulate.

Angelo J. Sanquedolce was a veteran of the Korean Conflict, a highly respected leader and a goodwill ambassador for the City. He leaves a proud, lasting legacy as a distinguished, innovative municipal official and compassionate humanitarian. Angelo J. Sanquedolce will forever be remembered and admired for his significant achievements, and for his devotion and faithfulness to duty, family, friends and community.

The Heritage Riverfront Park Plaza is hereby named and dedicated in honor of Angelo J. Sanquedolce, Comptroller of the City of Norwich from 1968 to 1998, for thirty years of exemplary public service, and for numerous and lasting contributions to the well-being of others, pursuant to a resolution adopted by the Norwich City Council on November 16, 1998. His professional and personal accomplishments, expertise and commitment to excellence established a lofty standard for all to emulate.

Angelo J. Sanquedolce was a veteran of the Korean Conflict, a highly respected leader and a goodwill ambassador for the City. He leaves a proud, lasting legacy as a distinguished, innovative municipal official and compassionate humanitarian. Angelo J. Sanquedolce will forever be remembered and admired for his significant achievements, and for his devotion and faithfulness to duty, family, friends, and community.

Italian Heritage Monument

Plaque sponsored by the Italian Heritage and Cultural Committee of Norwich

Located on 305 Broadway and Chelsea Parade

The Italian Monument to Christopher Columbus.

In anticipation of the 1992 planned celebrations of the upcoming 500th Anniversary of the discovery of America by Cristoforo Colombo as well as to honor our immigrant parents and other forbears, it was decided to have an obelisk monument erected on the green in front of the Norwich Free Academy. It was early 1990 when an active subcommittee was formed of the members of the Italian Heritage and Cultural Committee of Norwich. The monument was dedicated on October 11, 1992 as part of the yearlong celebration 500th Anniversary. Many members spent two years searching and locating the families, many of whom no longer reside in this area.

The 400 names of the families that contributed to this undertaking adorn the monument. The inscription reads:

CRISTOFORO COLOMBO
1492-1992
ONORATE I VOSTRI GENITORI
(Honor Thy Parents)

Chelsea Gardens
Located on Rockwell Street

Entrance to the Chelsea Botanical Gardens

Chelsea Gardens is an ambitious project aimed to bring a world-class, year-round, self-supporting botanical garden to 80 acres of prime natural land in Mohegan Park. It is located on Rockwell Street adjacent to Norwich Memorial Rose Garden. When completed it is expected to attract 100,000 annual visitors and employ up to 40 full and part-time persons. An already completed Master Plan envisions five development phases which will require an estimated 20 years to complete at around $80 million.

Chelsea Gardens is a non-profit organization consisting of a volunteer board of directors.

First Congregational Church

Located on 81 East Town Street

The First Congregational Church

This Church is the fifth meeting house erected in Norwich. The first meeting house, built around 1660, stood near the southeast corner of the Green. The second meeting house, erected in 1675, was on the summit of Meeting House Rocks and served as a lookout against Indian raids during King Philip's War. The third meeting house was built on the hill near the site of the old one and completed in 1713.

The fourth Church was built at the corner of the Green, completed in 1770 and consumed to ashes in 1801 by a fire of incendiary origin. The cornerstone of the present Church, the fifth, was laid on June 18, 1801, by General Ebenezer Huntington.

The existing building is representative of the period when the huge, barn-like structures of the 18th century were becoming more ornate. This is evidenced by the square two-story tower and projecting portico which repeats the rather flat lines of the roof and the corner quoins of the main building. The structure was extensively remodeled in 1845 and in later years.

Central Baptist Church

Plaque sponsored by members of Central Baptist Church
Located on Union Square

Old Central Baptist Church on lower Broadway

Current Central Baptist Church

Central Baptist Church was founded in 1840 and under the zeal and energy of Rev. Miner G. Clarke grew rapidly to over 400 members. The church's first organist, Ithamar Conkey, composed the music to "In the Cross of Christ I Glory" in 1849. William Howard Doane, the prominent hymn writer, was baptized in the church in 1851. The present edifice was constructed on this site in 1891 at a cost of $68,300 and in 1899, Bushnell Chapel, since replaced in 1978, was erected. The present Sunday school, known originally as the "Gilbert Property," was purchased in 1925 and subsequently joined to the church by an office wing, largely through the efforts of Charles D. and Charles F. Noyes. The cornerstone of the present building was laid in 1891, "that upon it may stand for years to come a temple that shall be open to all who desire to worship the God of our Fathers, whether they be rich or poor, high or low, home or foreign born, and without respect to races or conditions, all shall be alike, welcome."

First St. Mary's Church

Plaque sponsored by Philip J. Shannon
Located at the intersection of Central Avenue & North Main Street

The First St. Mary's Church.

ONCE UPON A TIME IN NORWICH, Irish immigrants fled to America to escape the "great hunger," the Irish potato famine. Before the famine, many Irish had already settled in Norwich in this area now known as Greeneville. They built shanties along the railroad tracks in what they termed "Twomeyville," and they earned the title of "Shanty Irish." They were employed in great numbers to build the Norwich & Worcester Railroad. The Irish brought with them Catholicism, and in the early 1840s, Father James Fitton held Mass among the shanties, for there were few permanent buildings.

By 1843, the Irish Catholic population had grown sufficiently to require a church. The first Roman Catholic church in Eastern Connecticut was in this very structure, consecrated in 1845, and remains a tribute to the settlers of Greeneville and the first St. Mary's parish. By 1853, the Catholic population had increased to over 4,000, and St. Mary's Church could no longer accommodate the many parishioners.

It was the Irish Catholics from Greeneville who funded the construction of St. Patrick's Church, which is today St. Patrick's Cathedral. This building was built to serve the first Catholic population in Norwich. Later, the Irish who fled the famine established themselves in their new world, Norwich. The Irish immigrant population later built for William Greene, about 1842, the mills in Greeneville where many were employed. Thereafter, the shanty town, "Twomeyville," was officially known as Greeneville.

A Norwich native and parishioner of St. Mary's, the Very Reverend William P. Brady was ordained and said his first Mass in this the original St. Mary's Church. He later went on to become President of St. John's College in Brooklyn, New York.

St. Patrick's Cathedral

Plaque sponsored by Mr. & Mrs. James P. Cronin
Located on 213 Broadway

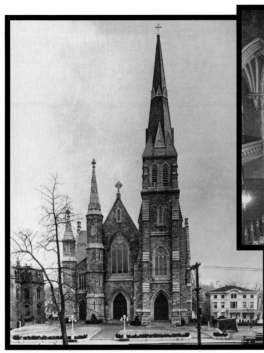

(left) St. Patrick's Church in the 1940s, with Dr. Kirby's home to the right, overlooks Broadway. Dr. Kirby's home would eventually be the diocesan office. (top) The old St. Patrick Church as it looked before it was renovated as a cathedral.

Once upon a time in Norwich…From its founding in 1659 through the 1700s, when Samuel Huntington and Benedict Arnold walked the byways of this city, and even after the election of George Washington as the new nation's first president, no Catholics lived in Norwich. Only after the War of 1812, in 1824, did Edward Murphy, the first Irish Catholic, take up residence.

In 1831, Father James Fitton administered the first baptism, and the first Catholic marriage occurred in 1840. The "great hunger," the potato famine in Ireland, brought the Irish immigrants to Norwich where they settled in shanties along the railroad tracks where they were employed to build the Norwich & Worcester Railroad.

The first Holy Sacrifice of the Mass was on December 25, 1844 at St. Mary's Church in lower Greeneville. By 1853, the Catholic population numbered over 4,000. In 1867, it was determined that another church was needed. Father Daniel Mullen, Pastor of St. Mary's, purchased this site, and on Good Friday, April 7, 1871, the work on St. Patrick's Church began. The Irish from Greeneville marched 1,700 strong, led by Dr. Patrick Cassidy, to the present site. Horses and carts, filled with picks and shovels, arrived with the workers, and from Good Friday morning to Easter Sunday the volunteer army dug the complete foundation by hand. Parishioners paid 10 cents a week and thus paid for the Gothic church. Father Shahan said the first Mass on a temporary altar on St. Patrick's Day, 1879.

The great hurricane of 1938 severely damaged the church. Undaunted, the pastor, Father Alexander F. Mitchell, led the restoration efforts and assured the parishioners the church would be returned to its former majestic presence, especially the beautiful St. Patrick window which had sustained significant damage. In 1950, Monsignor John J. Reilly, Director of the National Shrine of the Immaculate Conception, was assigned to St. Patrick's and given the task of renovating the Gothic church into a cathedral to become the seat of the Diocese of Norwich. The church was consecrated as a cathedral on September 2, 1952. His Holiness Pope Pius XII named the Most Reverend Bernard J. Flanagan of Burlington, Vermont as Norwich's first bishop.

Jewish Congregations & Community

Plaque sponsored by the Norwich Hebrew Home For the Aged
Located on High Street & the West Side

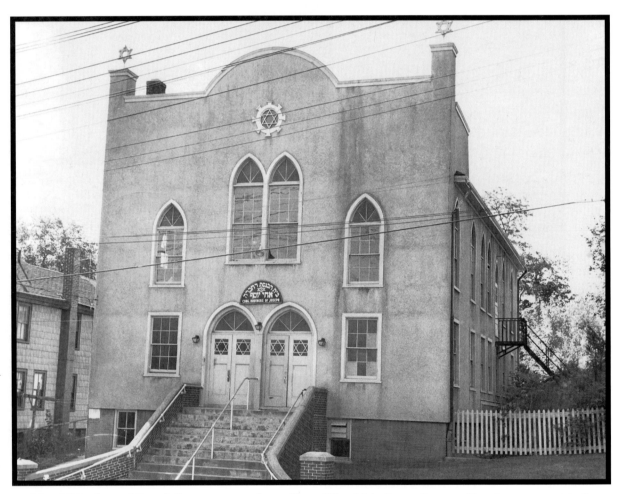

The old Brothers of Joseph Synagogue stood proudly on West Main Street. It was a historic monument to the Jewish community that first settled on the West Side.

Like other ethnic communities before it, High Street and the West Side became home to the Jewish community of Norwich from the late 19th century until the middle of the 20th century. The streets in this neighborhood teemed with small shops and peddlers that sold foods and goods, speaking principally Yiddish, the Jewish secular language of Europe. Kosher foods were readily available and the neighborhood closed down on Saturday in observation of the Sabbath.

The High Street Shul (Synagogue), a prominent synagogue among others in the neighborhood, were Orthodox establishments, featuring segregated seating for men and women, services in Hebrew exclusively, and sermons in Yiddish.

The Brothers of Joseph Synagogue

Plaque sponsored by the Norwich Hebrew Home For the Aged
Located on 2 Broad Street

The present Brothers of Joseph Synagogue on the corner of Broad and Washington Streets, built in 1964.

The Congregation was founded by Russian immigrant Jews in 1883, who unlike other predecessors, insisted all secular proceedings would be in Yiddish. A burial society was formed the same year. In 1884, the name Brothers of Joseph was adopted.

In 1898 their first permanent synagogue was built on West Main Street. The synagogue's first rabbi, in circa 1895, was Joseph Baron, believed to be the first full time rabbi to serve in Norwich. In 1909, he was succeeded by Rabbi Joseph N. Rosenburg, who served 42 years, until his passing in 1950.

In 1964, under the spiritual leadership of Rabbi Michael D. Geller, a new house of study and worship was built on the Osgood site at the corner of Broad and Washington Streets. The congregation moved from its 1898 West Main Street home.

St. Anthony's Chapel

Plaque sponsored by the Cape Verdean Community of Norwich
Located on 70 Central Avenue

St. Anthony's Chapel from the outside and inside.

Once upon a time in Norwich . . . Saint Anthony Chapel is rededicated to the memory of Joseph Candido Delgado born in 1882 on the island of Sao Nicolau, Cabo Verde and died June 1967. The chapel, a life-long dream of Joseph C. Delgado, was originally built and dedicated in 1926 at 165 Talman Street in Norwich to pay tribute to the patron Saint Anthony of Padua.

"I had a day dream one day and I saw the chapel and built it according to the picture which was presented to me at that time." – Joseph C. Delgado

St. Mary's RC Church the Parish of the Cape Verdean Community of Norwich and the Delgado Family join with the Cape Verdean community to dedicate this chapel as a symbol of faith on this Twenty-ninth day of April 2006.

Beth Jacob Community Synagogue 1929-1979

Plaque sponsored by the Norwich Hebrew Home For the Aged
Located on 100 Church Street

In the summer of 1929, twenty-nine Jewish families came together to found a more liberal congregation, The Norwich Jewish Community Synagogue. In 1934 the name was changed to The Beth Jacob Community Synagogue.

Principally first and second generation immigrants, from eastern Europe, these courageous Jewish pioneers wanted a more modern, American approach to their historic religion, one that would teach their children the heritage of their fathers while blending more seamlessly into the American landscape.

The new Conservative Jewish movement afforded this with its mixed seating of men and women, services in a blend of English and Hebrew, and sermons in English.

By 1979 the old church building was visibly worn and the Congregation built a new home at 400 New London Turnpike.

The old Beth Jacob Community Synagogue

Beth Jacob
Community Synagogue
1979-Present

Plaque sponsored by the Norwich Hebrew Home For the Aged
Located on 400 New London Turnpike

The present Beth Jacob Synagogue

For 50 years this United Synagogue of America Congregation (conservative movement) resided on Church Street in downtown Norwich. In 1975 a new secular administration was elected on a platform that it was time to relocate. The geographic dispersion of the congregation indicated a need to move closer to residential clusters and the needs of the congregation's activities begged for less, but more flexible space.

Between 1975 and 1979, this successful project was undertaken. The Beth Jacob Community Synagogue moved into its new home in September 1979.

Sacred Heart Church

Located on 156 Providence Street, Taftville

At first, the fire seemed controllable, but the entire church was destroyed before sundown. The beautiful marble altar with the arches and velvet drapes were totally destroyed by fire.

Taftville is a proud mill town. For generations its inhabitants arose and went home to the clanging of the bell at the gigantic Ponemah textile mill. But, for the village's large Roman Catholic population, the community's soul is found in its church bell.

The first Mass was celebrated in Taftville on St. Patrick's Day, 1873. Fitting, since the village that was largely to become French Canadian was first settled by the Irish, escaping famines in the homeland. Fitting, too, that Mass was said in Wequonnoc School, which was owned by the mill that brought Canadians to Taftville by the thousands in search of a better life.

Four years later, a small church was built by the hard work of its parishioners. It was the first of three churches at the present location to bear the name Sacred Heart in the small village. The first, dedicated in 1900, was little more than a basement with a roof. It was the very foundation for a major Ramanesque church that took 16 years to build.

Sadly, that edifice was destroyed by fire on a Sunday morning, April 29, 1956. The uncontrollable blaze burned for $4^1/2$ hours, consuming everything but the baptismal font and the bell tower.

A scant two years later, the present Sacred Heart Church was dedicated. A modern-looking church even a half-century later, the house of worship at the corner of Hunters Avenue and Providence Street is still the center of spiritual life for Taftville's active and changing Catholic population.

BILL STANLEY BOOKS
INCLUDE

Once Upon A Time – Book I

Once Upon A Time – Book II

Once Upon A Time – Book III

Only Yesterday

The Faith Jennings Collection

Once Upon A Time – Anniversary Edition

Backus Hospital Auxiliary – Audio Book

The 9-Mile Square*

*Won the Betty M. Linsley Award from the Association for the Study of Connecticut History, for the most important book on Connecticut history published in 2005.

Graphic Design Services By
Jesse F. Carbone – Carbone Graphics
328 Westchester Road
Colchester, CT 06415
1-860-908-0270
www.carbonegraphics.com

Printing Services By
Corporate Forms & Printing, Inc.
84 Sheffield Place
Southington, CT 06489
1-800-840-9945

All Bill Stanley Books Are Available At
Johnson's Flowers & Gifts
307 Washington Street, Norwich, CT 06360
(860) 889-1305

All books available to be shipped anywhere in the U.S. Shipping additional.